Setting Up Your Hair, Nail or Beauty Business

Setting Up Your Hair, Nail or Beauty Business

Julie Lee

Published by www.lulu.com

© Copyright Julie Lee 2017
Cover Image Copyright © Julie Lee 2017

SETTING UP YOUR
HAIR, NAIL OR BEAUTY BUSINESS

All rights reserved.

The right of Julie Lee to be identified as the author of this work has been asserted in accordance with the Copyright, Designs and Patents Act 1988.

No part of this publication may be reproduced, stored in a retrieval system, or transmitted, in any form or by any means, electronic, mechanical, photocopying, recording or otherwise, nor translated into a machine language, without the written permission of the publisher.

Condition of sale

This book is sold subject to the condition that it shall not, by way of trade or otherwise, be lent, re-sold, hired out or otherwise circulated in any form of binding or cover other than that in which it is published and without a similar condition including this condition being imposed on the subsequent purchaser.

ISBN 978-1-326-90666-5

Book formatted by www.bookformatting.co.uk.

Contents

Chapter 1 Introduction 1

About the Author 3
Acknowledgements 3
Huge, Heartfelt Thank Yous! 3
Introduction 4
Who is this Book For? 7
It's All About You...8
SWOT up! 10
Checklist 12

Chapter 2 Getting Started...13

How to Use This Book.......................................15
Plan of Action..16
Market Research...18
Business Mentors..22
Business Structure 23
Solicitors 25
Checklist 25

Chapter 3 The Business Plan 27

The Business Plan...29
Section 1: Executive Summary 30
Section 2: Your Business...................................31
Section 3: Legal Requirements 32
Section 4: Marketing...33
Section 5: Finances..34
Section 6: Financial Analysis, Financial Statements
and Projections 34
Business Plan Summary....................................35

Chapter 4 Finances – The Basics 37

Finances – The Basics 39
Raising Finance 40
Personal Survival Budget 42
Responsibilities 43
Understand Taxes 46
Financial Reports and book keeping 47
Checklist 48

Chapter 5 Making Money 49

Treatments and Services 51
Checklist 55

Chapter 6 Financial Forecasts 57

Financial Forecasts 59
Assumptions and Calculations 59
Sales Forecast 60
Cash Flow Forecast 60
Profit and Loss Forecast 61
Balance Sheet 61
Break-even Point 62
Return on Investment 62
Costing your Treatments 62
Share Distribution/Ownership 70
Revenue and Sales Forecast 71
Mobile/Home-based/Renting Space 71
For the Salon Owner 72
Assets 73
Checklist 73

Chapter 7 Location and Premises 75

So …where will you work from? 77
Opening a Salon 78
Checklist for Opening a Salon 82
Working from Home 82
Checklist for Home-based Workers 83
Going Mobile 83
Checklist for Mobile Workers 84
Renting Space for the Self-employed 85

Checklist for Renting Space for the Self-employed 86
Checklist 87
Business Rates 88
Utility Suppliers 88
Salon Design, Décor and Layout 89
Signage 91
Checklist 92

Chapter 8 Marketing and Promoting your Business 95

Your USP 97
Your Brand, Business Name and Logo 98
Marketing 100
Social Media 104
Website 106
Website and Graphic Designers 107
Design and Printing 107
Checklist 107

Chapter 9 Your business and the Law 109

Licences 111
Laws 112
Health and Safety 113
Insurance 116
Planning Permission 117
Checklist 118

Chapter 10 Running your Business 119

Paperwork 121
Salon Software 121
Choosing your Suppliers 122
Ordering Stock 122
Customer Complaints 124
Salon Rules for Staff 126
Rules for Clients 127
Making Appointments 127
Taking Money 128
Wages 128
Client Record Cards and Data Protection 130

Salon Operations Manual 130
Checklist 131

Chapter 11 Staff.. 133

The Recruitment Process...137
The Trade Test 140
The Interview 141
Induction Process 143
Staff Handbook 145
Employment Contracts...146
Final Note 148
Checklist 149

Chapter 12 Open Day 151

Create Some Hype..153
Simple Tips..153

Chapter 13 Keeping Motivated! 155

You CAN Do This! 157
Keeping Motivated...157
The Future...158
End Note 159

Chapter 14 Checklist 161

Chapter 1

Introduction

About the Author
Acknowledgements
Huge, Heartfelt Thank Yous,
Introduction,
Who is this Book for?
It's All About You
SWOT up

About the Author

Julie Lee is a full-time nail technician, beauty specialist, salon owner, educator, salon coach, multiple award-winning manicurist, session technician and mother of three.

After studying Beauty Therapy over twenty years ago, Julie began her career working for a close friend who offered her a job in his salon. From there, she accepted a role with a global beauty brand, whilst running her home-based nail and beauty business in her spare time.

After fifteen successful years, she was encouraged to pursue her dream of opening her first salon, and in 2006, The Nail Lounge opened its doors to the public.

"This book is dedicated to all the passionate entrepreneurs that have a dream of setting up their own business."

Acknowledgements

To Rory Blair for giving me a chance all those years ago.
To Louise Walsh for making me think big!
To Nick Grimshaw for his unrivalled business knowledge and support.
To my dear friend Janet Sillett for her incredible accountancy skills!
To iSalon business coach, Richard McCabe for teaching me how to work smarter, not harder.

Huge, Heartfelt Thank Yous!

To my wonderful parents Susan and Alan, for your never ending love and support.
To my beautiful sons Archie and Woody, for never complaining when Mum works!

To my equally beautiful daughter Jasmine – who is so proud of me, it touches my heart.

To my lovely sister Allison and brother-in-law Richard, for all your help with the children.

To my fabulous mother and father-in-law, Glen and Jim, for always helping out.

To my amazing team at The Nail & Beauty Lounge, for their hard work and loyalty over the years.

To Kelly, my manageress, PA, wing-lady and dear friend for making my life a simpler one!

To my wonderful friends Joanne, Tracey and Lisa …thank you for never doubting me, and for always listening to my (often crazy) ideas!

And last but not least, to my hard-working husband Richard, for supporting me in everything I do and for always keeping me grounded.

Introduction

So, you've taken the first step toward starting your very own business! May I be amongst the first to congratulate you on this brave decision, and wish you the very best of luck in the life-changing journey that lies ahead. It's such an exciting time and one that's sure to be packed with some of your most challenging and satisfying times yet.

When I first sat down to write this book, my aim was to guide people just like you through the complex, and often daunting process of opening a hair, nail or beauty business. I found it all entirely confusing to say the least! I just didn't know where to begin. I had a clear image in my head of what I wanted to achieve and how my salon would look, but the more I researched, the more confused I became. There were planning obligations to deal with, leases to negotiate, taxes to get my head around, health and safety requirements that I didn't understand, employment laws to learn and contracts to negotiate. The list seemed endless and I promised myself that one day I would put all my findings onto paper to help people just like you, in the simplest way possible.

So whether you're planning to hit the roads and go mobile, work from the comforts of your own home, rent a space within an established business, or indeed set up your very own salon - this book will guide you every step of the way.

Given that you're holding this book in your hands right now suggests you've already put some serious consideration into setting up your own business. And like many budding entrepreneurs, you might already have exciting ideas about where you'll be based, which treatments you'll be offering, and perhaps you've already decided what the sign will look like above the door!

So my first suggestion is to pop the kettle on, get yourself a brew, and go grab a pen and paper.

And now that you're sitting comfortably, let's begin by getting some of those brilliant ideas out of your head - and into your notebook.

However, before the pen hits the pad, close your eyes and take a moment to visualise your own successful business. What does it look like? What is the dream? Think about how it'll feel unlocking the door of your very own salon, and what you want to achieve by working for yourself. Maybe you want to start a small salon from your own home? Or perhaps you'd like to operate a mobile service and visit clients in their homes? You might want to keep things simple by renting space in an established salon or perhaps the dream is much bigger than that, and you aspire to run a multi-million pound franchise?

Allowing yourself to dream big and make it real via a few, simple bullet points will give you a genuine goal to work towards. And putting those dreams on to paper will give you something tangible to measure your progress against - which is far more likely to result in success than simply having pictures in your head.

By answering questions such as those above, and recording your notes in print, you'll have already made a start on your all-important Business Plan, so all we need to do next is start breaking those dreams down into smaller, more manageable goals and objectives.

Over the next day or two, treat yourself to a hard-backed notebook, and begin to jot down all your ideas and inspirations. Use it to log anything and everything from motivational quotes and logo ideas, through to clippings and cut-outs of stunning salons with beautiful décor.

My first tip is to write your dreams down in your notebook - and be sure to add to it often. You'll find it a constant source of inspiration and it'll help to keep your mind focused on the big picture, and your eye on the prize.

DARE TO DREAM – no idea is too big!

Whilst my own business is now well established, I still have dreams and aspirations about 'the next big thing'.

It was always my dream to write a book that would help others, as it once was to do the nails at London Fashion Week. I dreamed that I'd work for a global beauty brand, and that I'd be able to share my passion and knowledge for all-things nails and beauty through the recruitment and education of my very own team. I dreamed about opening a successful training arm to my business, and of owning a contemporary salon that offered bespoke treatments. And I'm proud to say that all those dreams have now been achieved …but, like yours, they don't stop there!

I still believe I can work toward making the rest of my dreams come true, and it's a philosophy that's served me well so far, providing all the fuel I need to keep motivated and focused. And no matter how big or small the dreams have been in the past, they all started off as a simple list of bullet points on a humble piece of paper.

As you start populating those bullet-points into your notebook, just imagine you're writing a Christmas wish-list for your new business, and over the course of the pages that follow, let's see if we can start turning those thoughts into things!

<u>Who is this Book For?</u>

There are predominantly two types of people in our industry:

The **artisans**, who are the skilled service providers such as hairdressers, nail technicians and beauty therapists, and the **entrepreneurs** - those with the business experience, knowledge or vision to turn a simple idea into a successful business.

If you feel you fit into either one of these categories, you'll already have the toolbox required to successfully run a business in the hair, nail or beauty industry.

Are you...

- a Hairdresser?
- a Beauty Therapist?
- a Nail Technician?
- an entrepreneur wishing to set up in one of the areas above?
- already established in the industry?

Do you...

- want to set up at home?
- want to go mobile?

- want to set up your own salon?
- want to rent space in an established salon?
- need a checklist to ensure that you have everything covered to successfully establish a business?

If you've answered 'yes' to any of these questions, then read on....

<u>It's All About You</u>

Starting your own business is an exciting time and if this has been your dream for a while, now's the time to make it happen!

'Entrepreneur' may sound like an ambitious title to give yourself, but entrepreneurs are just normal people with a business idea that just won't go away! Of course, there's so much more to setting up a business than simply having a good idea, and if you're seriously considering 'going it alone', you must be prepared to know that life will never quite be the same again.

Before we go any further, I really can't emphasise enough the serious impact that starting a business will have upon your life.

It isn't a decision to be taken lightly, and there are likely to be financial, physical and emotional strains along the way - particularly during the early phase, when you will undoubtedly sacrifice your time, relationships and social opportunities to get your business off the ground.

So start off by asking yourself **why you want to run your own business**? Will it give you the satisfaction and stimulation that you are looking for, and do you have the right skills and experience to make it work - not just in the short term, but for the rest of your career? It might be your motivation to work around your family commitments, or perhaps your business started off as a hobby, and now it feels like it's the right time to take it up to another level?

Whatever your reasons might be, be sure to clearly articulate them in your notebook; and if you ever find yourself asking why you're putting yourself through all the trials and tribulations of setting up your own business, you can always refer back to those initial reasons, which will provide you with the added impetus you need when the going gets tough.

> When I was setting up for the first time, I was fortunate enough to have the love and support of my husband, family and friends, who were always there to help me with everything from childcare to housework! **Don't ever underestimate the importance of a good support network!**

Now that you've decided **why** you want to run your business, you might be wondering what qualities you will need in order to drive your ideas forward?

For me, there are several characteristics that are absolutely essential, and if you're going to bring your business ideas to life, you'll need all of these in abundance...

- Determination and passion. These are vital ingredients for every successful person.
- Confidence - in order to negotiate deals and take measured risks.
- Communication skills - for building lasting relationships with your clients, suppliers and staff.
- Problem solving skills - as there'll be lots (and lots) of hurdles to jump!
- Organisational skills - whether it's diary management, book keeping, stock lists or financial forecasts – you'll need to be supremely organised at all times.
- A thick skin. The more successful you are, the more people may resent you for it - particularly in this cowardly age of social media. You may also come up

against people that mock your ambition or ideas, so stand tall, proudly puff out your chest and cut out any negative influences in your life.

SWOT up!

Whilst it's a relatively straightforward exercise, I found it really useful to do a personal SWOT analysis when I first started out.

This is a simple task that encourages you to identify your Strengths, Weaknesses, Opportunities and Threats, and will add real value to your business plan. To help you fill in your own personal SWOT analysis, have a go at answering the following questions:

Strengths

- What do you do better than anyone else?
- What skills and qualifications do you have?
- Are you involved in any networks? Think about your social circles as well as business contacts.
- Do you have good connections? Is there anyone that can lend advice, endorse your work, or publicise your business via local and social media?

Weaknesses

- Are you completely confident in your skills, or do you require some extra training?
- Is there anything you don't enjoy doing? (Such as paperwork, stocktaking, or any particular treatments?)
- Do you have any negative work habits? (Do you tend to be late or a little disorganised?)
- Is there any aspect of setting up your business that fills you with dread?
- Do you have an adverse credit history?

Opportunities

- Is your industry growing? If so, how can you take advantage of this?
- Are any of your local competitors failing to do something important?
- Do you hear people complain about others in your industry? If so, how could you use this to your advantage?
- Has a prime location or property recently become available?

Threats

- Could any of your weaknesses lead to threats in the future?
- Are your competitors providing a better standard of work than you?
- Are there lots of established salons in close proximity that offer the same services?
- How is the current economic climate? Do people have expendable income to spend on your services and products?

Strengths	Weaknesses
Opportunities	Threats

By completing your personal SWOT analysis you will now have a clearer understanding of each of these areas.

Identifying your strengths will clarify that you CAN do this, and by recognising your weaknesses you'll know exactly which areas you need a little help with, which, if you improve, will give you a much higher chance of success!

Checklist

- Write down your vision. What does your dream business look like?
- Write down WHY you want to run your own business, and ask yourself 'do I have the right skills?'
- Complete your own personal SWOT analysis.

Chapter 2
Getting Started

How to use this Book
The plan of Action
Market Research
Business Structure
Business Mentors
Solicitors

How to Use This Book

Firstly, this isn't a 'business book'. It was written to signpost you in the right direction and help you find a methodical way through the minefield of setting up your business. There are lots of great books and resources available to you once you're up and running, but this is the first stepping stone to getting you started.

I urge you to use the book as a checklist. Highlight relevant sections, make lots of notes, use the links, and tick off the parts you have done to keep you on track.

This book has been divided into fourteen chapters:

1. Introduction
2. Getting Started
3. The Business Plan
4. Finances – the Basics
5. Making Money
6. Financial Forecasts
7. Location and Premises
8. Marketing and Promoting your Business
8. Your Business and the Law
10. Staff
11. Running your Business
12. Opening Day
13. Keeping Motivated
14. The checklist

I have compiled a step-by-step Action Plan on page 17 with relevant page numbers to point you in the right direction.

Simply start at the top and work your way down the list, making sure you **complete each task that is relevant to you.** Each chapter has a checklist to keep you on track, together with suggested links to websites, downloads and templates - plus practical exercises for you to complete along the way.

Now let's begin…

<u>Plan of Action</u>

So where should you start? The process of setting up your own business can be an exciting but daunting one, and some aspects are far more fun and appealing than others. The design and décor, shopping for products and planning your treatment list are all stimulating examples, and it could be all-too-easy to ignore or put off some of the more 'boring' tasks …but DON'T!

Making sure that you've thoroughly completed all your research, planning and finances will make running your own business so much easier (and give you far less stress!) in the long run. It will allow you to establish your business and then in time, begin to grow it.

> Starting a business without a clear plan is like embarking on a very long journey without knowing where you're going! Consider your plan as a sat-nav, which takes you on the fastest, safest and most sensible route.

Below you'll find a brief overview of exactly what needs to be done, and you'll be pleased to know we'll be taking a deeper dive into all the detail as we work our way through the book. For easy reference, I've included all the relevant page numbers for you to check back at a later point.

1	Market research	Page 18
2	Start your Business Plan	Page 29
3	Work out your start-up costs	Page 39
4	Seek financing	Page 40
5	Find a Mentor	Page 22

6	Research available premises and make appointments for viewings	Page 77
7	Research all Laws and Regulations relevant to your business	Page 111
8	Find an Accountant	Page 44
9	Find a Solicitor	Page 25
10	Register your Company (if Limited)	Page 43
11	Open a bank account	Page 43
12	Secure finances	Page 40
13	'Complete' on your premises	Page 81
14	Arrange Business Rates	Page 80
15	Decide on staffing levels and advertise	Page 135
16	Plan your Treatment List	Page 51
17	Interview staff	Page 137
18	Begin your salon design and layout	Page 90
19	Instruct all utility suppliers	Page 88
20	Advertise to shout about what's coming!	Page 153
21	Source a Web Designer and begin your website design and build	Page 107
22	Set up Social Media accounts and begin campaign for friends and followers	Page 104
23	Write a salon procedures manual and job descriptions	Page 145
24	Apply for applicable licences	Page 111
25	Arrange all relevant insurances	Page 116
26	Start shop works, décor and shop fit. Order all equipment	Page 89
27	Get car signwritten if mobile	Page 91
28	Get all promotional materials designed and printed	Page 107
29	Complete all Health and Safety Policies and Procedures	Page 113
30	Order stock	Page 122
31	Plan and complete staff Induction	Page 143
32	Complete salon operations manual	Page 130
33	Clean and organise salon	
34	Plan your open/start day	Page 153

Market Research

Before you go any further, market research should be your first port of call. At this moment in time, you'd be forgiven for thinking you've stumbled upon the best idea in the world, but without some carefully considered research, you could be heading for real trouble.

For any new business to be a success, every aspiring entrepreneur must understand the marketplace they're operating within. Hair, nail and beauty businesses are not a new phenomenon after all, so in this respect, you must identify a way to make **your** business stand out from the rest. You'll also need to find out if there is the need for your services in the location you're thinking about trading in. You should use this opportunity to gather as much information as possible on your target market and your local competition, and to gather the thoughts of potential clients. There are a variety of ways you can do this, including desk research, or by creating a questionnaire and getting out there to seek invaluable local opinion.

First of all you need to think about your dream clients. Who are they? How old are they? Where do they eat? Where do they drink? What social activities do they take part in? What cars do they drive? How much money do they earn? Are they ladies who lunch or working Mums? Work out who it is you want to serve. Be as specific as possible with this and remember this - **we are not here to serve everybody.** Identifying your dream client will have a significant impact on everything from your décor to the treatments you will offer.

Once you are clear on your dream client, do some desk research. The internet can provide you with lots of information (mostly for free) and you can use it to find out who your competitors are, what they have on offer, how much they charge for their services, their proximity to your proposed location, and their social media presence. The web can also be used to find out more about your desired location, and to gather important statistics on your industry.

You could also create a questionnaire and get out there asking the public. The point in this exercise is to find out as much information from potential clients as possible.
When preparing your questions, think very carefully about the information you want to obtain; create a questionnaire around **your** business, ensuring you tailor all your questions around whether you'll be operating from home, going mobile, renting a space*, or owning your own salon.

Make sure you conduct your market research in and around the area you want to trade in and consider asking local business owners and staff for their thoughts and opinions too. If you're setting up in an established salon, spend time chatting to existing clients about the kind of treatments they currently go elsewhere to receive.

Another element worth considering would be to carry out your research at different times of the day. I remember getting very different responses from the people I interviewed in the evening than those I spoke to during the day – and perhaps that's because they had a little more time or were less stressed?

Do bear in mind of course, that the public are often wary about being stopped. Our first instinct is to think we're about to be sold something, so ALWAYS approach every situation with a warm smile and be polite at all times – after all, they may well be your future clients!

* If you're renting space in a salon offering the same services you'll be providing, market research is not necessary.

First of all you need to find out all about the **demographics**. This is the statistical information of your potential clients, such as their geographical location, age, gender, family status and occupation.

To find out more, you could ask:

1. Are they single or married?
2. Which salary bracket they're in?
3. Where they live?
4. Where they work?
5. Whether or not they're professional people, or perhaps stay-at-home parents?
6. Whether they're male or female?
7. Whether they're married, single or living with a partner?
8. Whether or not they have children?
9. Whether they're employed, self-employed, a student or unemployed?
10. Which age group they fall in to?

Your next task is to find out their **psychographics**, which refers to their personal behaviour, buying habits and lifestyle choices. To do this, you'll need to ask questions such as:

1. Whether or not they go to a local salon for beauty, hair or nail treatments?
2. Whether they have ever used a mobile nail technician, beautician or hairdresser?
3. And if not, why not?
4. Would they ever consider using a mobile professional as an alternative to a salon?
5. Which treatments they have on a regular basis? (include a tick-list of hair, beauty and nail treatments)
6. How much they pay on average for particular treatments, such as a cut and blow dry, a gel polish, a brow wax, a facial or a manicure?
7. How often they have these types of treatments done?
8. Which of these aspects are the most important to them: Customer service; price; quality; convenience; or luxurious surroundings?

9. How much they spend on average on hair, beauty and nail products each month?
10. Which magazines they read?
11. Their preferred make up brand?

> Remember, you must ask questions that are relevant to YOUR business.

Check with your council as you may need a licence to carry out questionnaires.

Analyse your data
Asking the questions is only a small part of this important task. To make the most of the information, you'll need to take the time to analyse the data to produce some meaningful conclusions. I already knew who my 'dream client' was. The information I collected proved to me that that client existed!

This then had an impact on everything to do with the look and feel of the salon, from the colour scheme and décor, to the logo and promotional materials. In essence, the data helped to define our BRAND – and therefore, the types of customers we were hoping to draw in.

By the time you've completed this exercise, you'll have a very clear picture of the types of people that might use your services, as well as key information about their spending habits, expectations, wants and needs.

You may well be surprised at the findings of your questionnaire, and may even decide to tweak your original plan off the back of your survey…

For example, an original plan for a very girly, hot pink salon soundtracked by the latest R&B hits might be in stark contrast to the results of your survey, which showed that the majority of your potential clients in the area are over the age of 50. Would your funky décor, fat bass lines and hot pink accessories prevent them from coming in?

Perhaps when conducting your desk research, you discovered there are twenty other salons within a ten mile radius offering the same proposition as you. Would this deter you, or would you have the confidence to take them on by offering something even better? If so, would you need to amend your Business Plan, and the financials around it to execute this ambition?

Either which way, once you've completed your market research, you can feed it into your Business Plan, and begin to use the findings to execute your marketing strategy.

<u>Business Mentors</u>

Business Mentors are usually people with extensive business experience, or those with a specific skillset in certain aspects of business, such as marketing or finance. They can bring a fresh eye to proceedings, and can offer you a wide range of help and advice, from helping you out with your Business Plan to guiding you through the dense forest of financial forecasts. They have a wealth of information they can share with you, and take great pride in adding successful business start-ups like yours to their CVs.

Why would I need one?
Unless you have prior experience of running a successful business, I do not see any negatives to recruiting a Mentor!

How and where would I get one?
Simply search 'Business Mentors' on the internet, and you should see a reasonable list of contacts in your local area. If you're applying for grants, funding or business loans, or if you're opening a bank account, a mentor may even be assigned to you as part of the package (see page 44).

When completing my SWOT analysis, I identified financial forecasting and a lack of Health and Safety knowledge amongst my weaknesses …I just didn't know where to start!

My Business Mentor helped me no end with these aspects, and for that, I will be forever grateful.

Business Structure

One of the key decisions you'll make is which legal structure to use.

This will depend on a number of factors ranging from the number of owners your business will have, the risks associated with your business, and its liability and tax commitments.

There are three types of business status in the UK, so you will need to decide if you are going to be a Sole Trader, a Partnership or a Limited Company. You should seek advice from your accountant, business advisor or solicitor on this, as they will explain the most suitable structure for you. For quick reference, I've included a brief overview of each below…

Sole Trader
This is the simplest way to run a business, and as a Sole Trader you will trade under a registered business name.

You and the business 'are one', and therefore, you'll be personally responsible for all liabilities - both financial and contractual. You must notify HMRC within three months of starting your venture (or face a financial penalty), and should open a business account to keep your personal and business finances separate.

Partnership
Finding a business partner with relevant skills and knowledge enables you to focus on the things you're best at.

For example, you might be an incredibly talented beauty therapist, but you may have very limited knowledge of finances and marketing. To remedy this, you could enlist a suitable business partner with skills in these areas.

In any Partnership, you MUST have a written agreement prior to trading - setting out each person's roles and responsibilities within the business – which will help to avoid all sorts of potential problems further down the line. Ask your solicitor to give this agreement a once over.

Limited Company
Although there are different types of Limited Companies, the most common is a Private Limited Company.

This type of structure means that the company is responsible for its own dealings and finances which are completely separate to your own personal finances. However, please be aware that both you and your spouse will be credit checked.

Profits made by the Limited Company after Corporation Tax has been paid will be owned by the company - but are then available to share with 'members' or Directors. Members are the people or organisations that own shares in the Limited Company.

Directors are the people who are responsible for managing the Limited Company and will often own shares - but they don't have to.

There are many legal responsibilities involved with being a Director and running a Limited Company, so be sure to speak to your solicitor, business advisor or accountant for more advice on this.

Solicitors

It is important to choose a solicitor with relevant knowledge and experience to suit your needs. They can advise you on typical issues and risks that your business might face, and are essential when entering into a lease or mortgaging a property. They can also give you excellent advice on employment law, should you need to employ staff.

I suggest you go off local recommendations when searching for a Solicitor, but be sure to get a price for their services prior to any work being carried out. However, a mobile, home-based or self-employed tenant should not need the services of a solicitor, as these types of business are relatively straight forward to set up.

More information to help you decide on your business structure is available at
www.gov.uk/business-legal-structures

Checklist

Read through the Plan of Action.
Do your desk research on competitors, the market and the industry.
Compile and conduct your questionnaire.
Look for a Business Mentor.
Find a solicitor if you need one.
Decide on your business structure.
Feed this into your Business Plan.

Chapter 3
The Business Plan

The Business Plan
Section 1: Executive Summary
Section 2: Your Business
Section 3: Legal Requirements
Section 4: Marketing
Section 5: Finances
Business Plan Summary

The Business Plan

It's one thing dreaming of owning your own business, but converting those dreams into a reality takes careful research and LOTS of planning! To help you do this, you'll need to get started on a clear Business Plan.

A Business Plan helps to clarify your thoughts and ideas, and can act as a working document that you'll be able to refer to (and continue to tweak) throughout the initial set-up, and during the operation of your business. It'll help you spot potential problems and mitigate their risk, and it'll be an extremely useful benchmark to monitor your progress against a cost-dependent schedule. It's also an ESSENTIAL requirement if you require funding.

Writing your Business Plan can seem a little overwhelming at first, but it needn't be complex. I would suggest it'll take you around two to three weeks to complete, but of course, that all depends on the number of hours you're able to dedicate to it each day. Although you'll start off with a blank piece of paper, you'll probably surprise yourself with the quality of document you end up producing.

A comprehensively produced Business Plan clearly illustrates you've carefully considered every aspect of your business, and the process you go through in completing this document will give you a much higher chance of success.

How to do it

There are a number of different resources available to help you write your Business Plan, including Business Mentors, detailed books and manuals, and via simple searches of the web. To save you some precious time though, I've put together a simple six-step guide that you can use to formulate your very own. As a rule of thumb, your Business Plan should be no more than around seven pages long, so try not to stress too much about it. Go to the relevant sections in the book for help on completing each task.

Section 1: Executive Summary

Your Executive Summary provides an 'at a glance' snapshot of your Business Plan.

Whilst it's the most crucial (and probably the most interesting) element of your Business Plan, it's perfectly acceptable to present your information as simple bullet points. This will ensure all the key facts and figures leap out from the page, and it'll also make your proposals much easier for the reader to digest. Perhaps aim to complete all of your bullet points in less than a hundred words.

The Executive Summary will be positioned on the first page of your finished document, although it'll actually be the very last section you'll complete.

Remember, financial institutions and potential investors will be reading this opening gambit, so take time to pull out the key 'headlines', ensuring that your bullet points are both exciting and make perfect business sense. Bear in mind the huge importance of pitching this section just right, as it is often the only part of your Business Plan the banks or potential investors will read before skipping straight through to the financial section.

The best way to approach your Executive Summary is to ask yourself the following question:

If you only had one page to explain your new business to a stranger, what would you say?

This is a prime opportunity to tell the reader how unique your business is, and how passionate and qualified you are to make it a success …and make a financial profit!

It should consist of the following details:

Name of the business
Description of the business
Location
Projected revenue
Start-up costs
Funds required
The future
Competitors
Keys to success
Contact details

Section 2: Your Business

This section will tell the reader who you are, what you're planning on doing and how you'll go about doing it. This part of your plan should be reasonably straightforward to complete, but be sure to include at least a sentence on each topic.

Business Name/Logo	What is your business going to be called?	
Contact Details	How will people reach you? Telephone number Email address Website	
Business Address	Where will you run your business from?	
Business Structure	Will you be a Limited Company, a Sole Trader or in Partnership?	
Business Description	A brief but exciting description of your business.	
Business History	Is this a new business or have you already been trading?	
Products and Services	Which treatments and products will you be using and selling?	

Management and Staff	Who will manage and work in your business. What will their roles be?	
Premises and Location	Where will your business be located and where will you work from?	
Shop fit furniture and Decoration	Document the set-up costs. This will help you establish your budget.	
Suppliers	Who will your suppliers be? Have contacts and provisional contracts been made?	
Opening Hours	What will your trading hours be?	
SWOT Analysis and USP	What are your strengths, weaknesses, opportunities and threats? What is your unique selling proposition?	

Section 3: Legal Requirements

Write down what steps you have taken to ensure the business is legally compliant and its activities are protected.

Have you registered with HMRC?
Have you obtained all insurances?
Has the lease agreement been checked by a solicitor?
Have you obtained your special treatments licence?
Have you obtained planning permission?
…and have any other legal dependencies been organised?

<u>Section 4: Marketing</u>

This section of your Business Plan reflects your understanding of the market and industry, and how you will go about promoting your business.

Summary of the Marketing Plan	Document a summary of your intended marketing strategy and promotions. Write about your industry, who the target market are and how you will attract customers.	
Your Brand	What message are you trying to get out there? How will you create a presence in order to gain and maintain interest?	
Uniqueness	What makes your offer truly unique to your competitors?	
Your Customers	Who are they? How old are they? Where do they live? Provide the answers to these questions and any other information you have about them.	
Customer Loyalty	How will you reward customers for their loyalty?	
Competitor Analysis and SWOT	Who are your competitors, and how will you be setting yourself apart from them? Present the SWOT analysis on your competitors.	
Marketing Budget and Targets	How much will you spend on marketing your business? Will there be an on-going marketing budget?	
Schedule of Planned Promotions and Advertising	When and how will you run promotions? How will you monitor how successful these have been?	

Section 5: Finances

In this section you'll explain how much investment you need, how the invested money will be spent, and when you are planning to pay it back.

Proposed Financing	Where is your start-up money coming from and how much do you need?
Ownership and Return on Investment	If you need investors, what will their involvement be and how will you repay them?
Use of Proceeds	How will you allocate your money?
Reporting	How will you produce reports for investors in the business?
Investor Involvement and Payment of Fees	What do you want from your investors? If fees need to be paid to your investors, be sure to document them.

Section 6: Financial Analysis, Financial Statements and Projections

This section provides a complete breakdown of all of your estimated finances.

Start-up Costs	Equipment, machinery, furniture, fixtures and fittings.	
Start-up Costs	Premises/rent, insurances, legal fees and accountancy fees.	
Cash Flow Forecast	Your cash flow forecast for the next three to five years.	
Profit and Loss	Your P&L forecast for the next three to five years.	
Break even Figure	How much do you need to make to break even?	

Estimations and other Calculations	Show how you have estimated your predicted takings and how you came to that figure.	
Revenue	How are you going to make money? How much do you think you'll make?	
Costing Strategy	Work out the actual costs of your treatments.	

Business Plan Summary

Congratulations! By completing your Business Plan you should have a clear understanding of whether your business will be profitable and how you'll actually be able to achieve this.

Chapter 4

Finances – The Basics

How Much Money will you Need?
Raising Finance
Personal Survival Budget
Bank Account
Professional Help
Taxes and VAT
Financial Reports

Finances – The Basics

In this section, we'll look at the money you'll need to set up your business, your financial responsibilities as a business owner, and who to turn to for help with your finances.

How much money will you need?
The amount of money you will need to start up the business will vary depending on the size of the operation.

If you decide you'd like to work from home, go mobile or rent a space in an existing salon, your costs will of course be significantly reduced.

Depending on your premises, you will need to consider the following:

• Deposit
• Rent (possibly 3 months in advance)
• Business Rates
• Solicitor's fees
• Website set-up fee and running costs
• Limited Company registration fees (if applicable)
• Insurance fees
• Licensing fees
• Telephone line installation costs and line rental
• Broadband line rental
• A desktop computer or laptop
• A printer
• Computerised booking programme (if required)
• Stationery (price lists, appointment cards, gift vouchers etc.)
• Shop fitting costs
• All equipment
• Stock

• Ventilation and extraction system (nails)
• A vehicle (if mobile)
• Card machine or mobile payment technology
• A till or cash drawer

Raising Finance

You might need a significant pot of money to start your business, but where is it all going to come from? There are a number of options available…

Self-funding
Self-financed business ventures may come from a generous partner or your own personal savings. Be careful not to put your entire nest egg on the line though, as you'll need to limit the risks involved in setting up a business. You may need to postpone holidays and new cars until your business takes off, but in doing so, you'll be safeguarding your personal assets should the business fail.

Family and friends
When it comes to helping make your wishes come true, you may even find that your nearest and dearest are willing to put their faith in you and loan you the money.

If that's the case, make sure you have a written agreement to cover all parties. It should always include all aspects of what's been agreed, such as when and how much you've agreed to pay back, including any additional interest repayments.

This was actually how I was able to open my first salon, as I was lucky enough to have two wonderful friends who believed in my Business Plan …and trusted me enough to part with (and pay back!) their money. Between us, we worked out a sensible arrangement that took into account how much I could realistically afford to pay back each month, and I simply set up a standing order to reimburse them as per the written agreement.

Of course, the down side of borrowing money from friends and family is that it has the potential to destroy relationships should you fail to repay the money back. The lender may also want a stake in your business, which equates to a share in your profits once the business gets going - so be sure to cover all eventualities in your written agreement. You should also be aware that people who put their money forward may think they have a right to say how the business is run ...but you might have other ideas!

Bank loan
This is where your Business Plan will come into its own, so if you're considering applying for a bank loan, make sure it stacks up, as they'll need to know you've done your homework and that the business is a viable proposition. Essentially, the bank will want to know what every penny is being used for, how and when it will be repaid, and what securities you are able to offer.

Grants and Government Schemes
There are many private organisations and government-backed schemes that offer grants or loans for business start-ups, and each come with their own specific criteria which can be based around your age or the industry you are working in.

Search the internet for business start-up grants, or type 'Finance and Support for your Business' in the search bar at www.gov.uk

If you are between the ages of 18 and 30, the Prince's Trust could also be an option. Visit them at www.princes-trust.org.uk to find out more.

Funding Circle
The Funding Circle also offer accessible business loans. Based on your Business Plan, investors compete with each other to lend you money – which means you get to pick the best interest rates

possible! Find out more at www.fundingcircle.com.

Business Angels

Business Angels are wealthy individuals who invest their own money in start-up companies. Find out more by visiting the British Business Angels Association at www.ukbusinessangels association .org.uk/ or the Angel Investment Network at www.angelinvestment network. co.uk.

This option is probably better suited to those who are registering as a Limited Company, as the investor will almost always want shares in the business they are investing in.

Credit cards

If you are disciplined with money management and have a good credit history, a credit card might be an option. There are often great deals available with low interest rates.

> **Remember – if you want to borrow money for your business, you need to be a great ambassador for it! Make sure your enthusiasm and professionalism comes across in your Business Plan, and all dialogue.**

<u>Personal Survival Budget</u>

Once you've worked out how much your business will cost to start up, consider how much money you need to keep afloat. Fill in a monthly expenses sheet like the one below to figure out the costs you'll need to cover whilst your business gets going.

Monthly payments	A	Personal Expenses	B
Rent/mortgage		Entertainment	
Council Tax		Clothes	
Food/groceries		Gym	
Life Insurance		Eating out	
Home Insurance		Travel	

Monthly payments	A	Personal Expenses	B
Car payments		Charitable donations	
Car Fuel		Childcare	
Car Insurance		School dinner money	
Loan/Card repayments		Pet expenses	
TV Licence		Children's activities	
Satellite/Cable TV		Personal grooming	
Mobile phone		Lottery	
Bank charges			
Gas			
Electric			
Water Rates			
Home phone			
Broadband			
Childcare			
House maintenance			
Household supplies			
Other			

<u>Responsibilities</u>

As a business owner you have a responsibility to conduct your finances appropriately and within the law, so…

Set up a Bank Account

Banks are eager for your business, so shop around for the best deals. Every bank will have a business pack (usually full of useful information) with details of their fees. There are very often incentives such as 'free business banking for one year' for start-ups, so look around and search the internet. If you've decided to operate as a Limited Company, you should register with Companies House **before** setting up your bank account.

Find out:

- What their standing charges are
- If they provide telephone and internet banking
- If a free-of-charge Business Mentor is available
- What their overdraft arrangement fees are
- What rates of interest they offer
- Which supplier they suggest for taking card payments
- If they offer a service that accepts payments via a mobile phone

Once you've found the right bank for you, be sure to organise an overdraft facility on the account. The cost of arranged borrowing is far less expensive than unarranged borrowing, so it's a no-brainer!

Find out who can help you
You may wish to enlist the help of a professional book keeper or accountant (and in some cases both) to help keep you on track with your finances.

Book keepers can:
Record financial transactions
Post debts and credits
Produce invoices
Reconcile bank account
Maintain and balance subsidiaries, general ledgers and historical accounts
Prepare and complete your VAT returns
Complete your payroll (if you are employing staff)

Accountants can:
Complete all functions of a bookkeeper (as above)
Prepare, maintain and audit your financial records
Advise you on and organise your Tax
Submit your accounts to HMRC (statutory accounts, annual return,

VAT, Self-Assessment, Corporation Tax, PAYE etc.)

Advise on offsetting your expenses against Corporation Tax

Legally declare dividends (if Limited Company)

Help with budgeting and forecasting cash flow

Advise on credit control

Advise ways to arrange additional finance that could help to grow your business without risking it

Manage your end-of-year Profit and Loss accounts

> Ask family and friends for recommendations as there are some lazy, incompetent accountants out there! Believe me, I know.
>
> Worryingly, anyone can call themselves an accountant as the term isn't legally protected, so be careful who you choose. The term 'Chartered Accountant' however, IS protected - so I suggest you err on the side of caution and go with one of these.
>
> The best advice I can give you is choose an accountant THAT SPEAKS PLAIN ENGLISH and make sure that you always get a clear price for the services you require **before** any work is carried out.

Doing it yourself

If you are a Sole Trader, you may decide to do your own book keeping and submit your own Tax Returns. This can be relatively simple for one-man-bands, so if you think you're up to the job, go for it! I would suggest ordering a copy of 'Refreshingly Simple Finance for Small Business' by Emily Coltman on Amazon, which is packed with simple, easy-to-read advice.

There is also lots of useful information available at www.gov.uk.

> The very thought of doing my own books filled me with fear! I was not qualified or experienced in any aspect of accountancy but understood the legalities of proper accounting, and therefore employed a professional.
>
> My accountant is a constant source of information and helps to keep all the financial aspects of my business legal. This is money extremely well spent as far as I'm concerned.

<u>Understand Taxes</u>

As a UK business owner you are responsible for paying tax on your profits and earnings, and below is an overview of the most relevant taxations for small businesses. A common mistake new business owners make is failing to put their tax aside from their takings, thus leaving them with a tax bill to pay and nothing to pay it with. Getting into the habit of taking this out, whether it be daily, weekly or monthly and putting it into a separate account will ensure there are no nasty surprises when the dreaded tax bill arrives.

Personal Income Tax
If you're self-employed, in a partnership, or a Director of a Limited Company, you will need to complete self-assessments tax returns once a year.

Corporation Tax
If you own a Limited Company, Corporation Tax is payable on your taxable income or profits.

VAT
VAT is a tax you collect on behalf of the government and can make a difference to the price of goods or services you sell. Find out what the current VAT limit is to see if you need to register with HMRC. Your accountant can advise you on this.

> Remember that you must keep receipts for everything you purchase from equipment to products, as you may be able to offset these costs against any profit you make.

National Insurance Contributions

Although not officially a 'tax', these contributions are paid by both workers and employers towards the cost of certain benefits. Check current NIC rates at www.hmrc.co.uk.

Financial Reports and book keeping

Leaving paperwork to pile up can be the bane of any business owner's life. Decide on a suitable method for 'doing your books' and get into the habit of recording this information daily, weekly or monthly -whichever suits you best.

Your books will show you and your accountant exactly what money is coming in (incomings) and what is going out (outgoings). HMRC say that, at a minimum, sole traders and partnerships (not registered for VAT) must *'keep a record of all your sales and takings and all your purchases and expense'*. This is to allow you to fill in your tax returns fully and accurately. These records must be kept for five years.

For this you will need to:

- Keep a record of all sales
- Record all purchases
- Keep all bank statements

Depending on the size of your business, your book keeping can be anything from a book that you write your incomings and outgoings in (for a one-man-band) to a computer software package such as Microsoft Excel or SAGE (although the latter can be complicated unless you know what you're doing!)

I suggest you arm yourself with lots of files, dividers and lever arch files to keep your paperwork organised. To start you off, have one each for:

- Bills Paid (you can store each 'type' of bill in separate files i.e. utilities, supplier invoices etc.)
- Bills Unpaid
- Bank statements
-

In the hair, nail and beauty industry, payment for treatments are often in cash. It can be very easy to lose track of your accounts, so make sure you record everything when the transaction takes place.

<u>Checklist</u>

Work out your start-up costs.
Decide where the money will come from.
Work out your personal survival budget.
Research and set up a bank account.
Decide if you need an accountant or book keeper and find one.
Buy lots of files and label them!
Have a basic understanding of your Tax responsibilities.
Be aware of the financial reports you will produce.

Chapter 5
Making Money

Treatments and services
Retail
Renting out space
Special events
Website and apps

There are several ways to make money in your business - some more obvious than others. However, the key here is to be as creative as possible, and not to rely too heavily on your treatments alone!

Treatments and Services

This is the most obvious way to make money, as you will receive payment in return for the treatments you provide.

Your treatment list
Begin by writing down a list of all the treatments you'll be offering, together with the optimum length of time it takes to perform each of them. When allocating timings to your treatments, be mindful that they need to be financially viable, yet long enough for the treatments to be correctly performed. If you allow too long for appointments, it'll impact heavily on your profit margin, whilst rushing them will result in inadequate treatments and a poor customer experience.

The best way to plan your treatment list is to group them into categories of service, such as nails, waxing and colouring.

Here's a basic list of standard treatments and timings for you to use as a starting point.

Nails
File and polish	15 minutes
Full set of enhancements	60 minutes
Deluxe manicure	60 minutes
Gel polish	30 minutes

Beauty
Full facial	60 minutes
Spray tan	15 minutes
Body wrap	60 minutes
Full leg wax	30 minutes

<u>Hair</u>

Cut and blow dry	45 minutes
Hair extensions (full head)	4-5 hours
Treatment	15 minutes
Hair relaxing	60 minutes

Retail products

This is an area of your business that should never be overlooked.

Products can have a much higher profit margin than treatments, so you'll have the opportunity to make more money with far less time and effort. For example, if you take a standard facial or a massage, it'll cost an hour of your time - charged at, say, fifty pounds. Meanwhile, the same amount of money could be made in a moment, simply by selling a couple of cleansers!

As part of your service, you will (hopefully) provide every client with professional aftercare advice, so it's important that you retail all the products you recommend – and that you always have them in stock. If you don't have that cuticle oil, moisturiser or hair treatment the client feels is essential to maintain their 'just got out of the salon' look, they'll simply buy it from someone who does, or even worse, find it cheaper somewhere on the internet! So don't waste this golden opportunity to make some relatively easy money.

If your salon is likely to have staff, ensure they receive adequate training on all the products you'll be selling. You could even set retail targets for each member of your team, and incentivise them via commission payments on the sales.

Even mobile professionals should carry a small retail range with them at all times, to be absolutely sure an opportunity to make a sale is never missed.

A friend of mine specialises in facials and makes TWICE as much money selling products than she does doing the treatments. That's certainly something well worth thinking about!

If you want to be taken seriously as a hair, nail or beauty professional, I advise steering clear of 'gimmicky' products and companies. Your clients will be constantly asking your advice on new products and treatments, but will soon lose faith if you're suggesting the latest fad every month. Invest in quality treatments and products that actually work ...and your clients will love you for it!

Your retail area
Your retail area should be as enticing as possible in order to woo your clients and encourage them to buy those all-important extras. Depending on the size of your premises, it can be anything from beautiful, bespoke cabinets to a couple of well-appointed shelves behind your reception desk. Either way, your products must always offer a definite aura of desirability.

To do this, make sure you have some carefully selected products on display that are perfectly relevant to your customers; there's little point in selling clip-in hair extensions if the vast majority of your clients are the over fifties. You should also update your retail space each and every month to maintain the interest of your regular clients, and always keep your products dust-free, clean and clearly priced.

If you're planning on having a reception desk, why not have a selection of products under £10 on the counter (such as lipsticks, hair brushes, travel-sized products, cuticle oils, nail treatments and lip-gloss), alongside one of your beautifully presented gift cards?

> My biggest bug-bear are fluorescent stars, emblazoned with hand-written prices! These certainly don't go hand-in-hand with the beautiful, stylish salon you're aspiring to create.

Renting out space

If you work from your own salon or home, you could consider renting out space to generate other streams of income. Lash technicians, semi-permanent makeup artists, aesthetic practitioners and reflexologists are amongst the plethora of professionals who might be on the look-out for a reputable business to work from.

If you are considering renting out space, choose wisely and only deal with insured professionals you'd like to be associated with. You should always agree in advance whether you will take a percentage of their takings or a fixed fee for renting out your space, and ensure that you discuss and write up terms and conditions to be agreed and signed by all parties.

You should also check with your local council to ask if a special treatment licence is required, and be sure to let your own insurance provider know whenever a new freelancer begins to work on your premises.

Special events

Another way to generate income could be to host monthly events. Examples include make-up demonstrations, styling demo's for clients to recreate 'looks' using the latest gadget or product or an introduction to your latest treatment range. You could either sell tickets for these events, or use them as a tool to generate a buzz around your business, and make money through retail products further downstream.

Website and Smartphone apps

If you want to take your retail to another level, you could always add an online shop to your website.

There are a number of third party providers including Shopify and PayPal that will allow you to add a shopping cart to your site for a small fee. These applications allow customers to shop on responsive platforms, so that your website is easy to navigate on a PC, Mac, tablet or smartphone. There are also many app developers who will create a template specific to your business, which will allow your clients to purchase products, make appointments and search general information including your opening times, prices and location.

> Repeat business is crucial in our industry. It is far more difficult to gain new clients than to retain the ones you already have, so look after those who show loyalty to you, and they'll hopefully keep on coming back!
> Be sure to provide excellent treatments, great aftercare advice and exemplary customer service - always.

Checklist

Start thinking of different ways to generate income.

Write down your treatment list and timings.

Compile a list of retail products. Think of the profit!

Look at renting out your workspace.

Check out freelancers reputation and credentials before you commit!

Consider your retail area when designing your salon.

Find a web/app designer and find for inspiration for your website.

Chapter 6

Financial Forecasts

Introduction
Sales Forecast
Cash Flow
Profit and Loss
Estimations and Calculations
Balance Sheet
Break-even Point
Return on Investment
Costing Treatments
Direct and Indirect Costs
Share Distribution and Ownership
Revenue and Sales (including Targets)
Assets and Depreciation

Financial Forecasts

A financial forecast is a realistic estimate of your projected income and expenses. This crucial piece of work will give you and your investors a clear idea of whether your business is likely to be a profitable one, so it's certainly a worthwhile investment of your time.

Good forecasting will significantly reduce the risks involved in setting up your business, as a lack of planning and proper financial control is the most common reason that business start-ups fail. Your financial forecasts are not only a critical component of your Business Plan, but they're essential for your own peace of mind too, as they'll provide you with an inner confidence that your business is likely to turn a profit.

I don't expect every budding entrepreneur to have a maths or accountancy degree, so you'll be pleased to know that you don't need one for forecasting! However, it is very important that you have a basic understanding of your business finances at the very least, as this'll assist you in making sure your business is profitable, and doesn't risk running at a loss.

If you feel you need some additional support, accountants and business mentors can help, although I highly recommend you have a go yourself. After all - only you will know your business and its potential. Just take your time, but above all, don't put off doing your financial forecasts.

Assumptions and Calculations

Predicting the finances for your new business is not an easy task as much of it will be based on guesswork.
When you are making assumptions or calculating figures, you need to make make sure they're both **realistic** and **achievable**. Once you have worked them out, you'll include all these figures in your

business plan to show how you've calculated your financial forecasts.

In this section, we'll go through all the forecasts you'll need to complete, but when you get a spare moment, please also take a look at this short video at www.gov.uk/forecast-business-finances.

Your financial forecasts will consist of the following components:

- Sales forecast
- Cash flow
- Profit and loss
- Balance sheet (for larger businesses)
- Breakeven calculation
- Return on investment

Sales Forecast

Your sales forecast will illustrate your projected sales, month by month, so start off by working out **how many clients you aim to see each day and how much you expect them to spend**. To keep this simple, multiply this by the number of days you will work per week, and you'll be able to work out how much you might make in a month. Be realistic as you won't be busy 100% of the time, so build in contingency for quiet days, breaks, down-time and holidays.

Once these figures have been defined, you can use them as a basis for your cash flow and profit and loss forecasts.

Cash Flow Forecast

Your cash flow forecast indicates the cash that will be moving in and out of your business. The most basic way to represent a cash flow forecast is by using a simple spreadsheet that documents the monthly income and a breakdown of your business costs.

It can help you get a view of when upcoming cash shortages or surpluses may be, which will be most helpful when it comes to making financial decisions such as planning for your annual tax payments or helping you budget for new equipment. It will also help you identify how your business will cope if you hit hard times, allowing you to plan solutions in advance.

For your Business Plan, you should present a cash flow forecast for a period of up to three to five years.

For help with completing a cash flow forecast, or to download templates, visit https://www.startuploans.co.uk/cash-flow-forecast/.

Profit and Loss Forecast

A completed profit and loss forecast demonstrates the projected financial performance of your business over a period of time (either monthly or annually), and establishes whether you're likely to make or lose money. From here, you will then be able to set yourself sales targets based on your profit and loss estimates. To complete this you'll need to estimate your sales figures, for both your treatment and retail transactions, and also your predicted outgoings.

If you need help with completing a profit and loss forecast, you can download a template at http://smallbusiness.co.uk/profit-and-loss-template-20736/

Balance Sheet

A balance sheet or statement is a summary of the financial balances of a business. It is often described as a snapshot of a company's financial condition, and is made up of three parts: assets, liabilities and ownership equity.
Your book keeper or accountant can help with this.

Break-even Point

The break-even point of your business is reached when the total income matches the total costs and your business is neither making a profit or a loss. Anything above your break-even point is profit.

Return on Investment

The purpose of calculating the ROI is to measure the rates of return on money invested in a business.

To produce these financial forecasts, you would need to work out your:

- Direct/Indirect costs
- Share distribution/Ownership (for Limited companies)
- Revenue and sales
- Assets

Costing your Treatments

Now that you've made a decision on the treatments you'll be offering, you'll need to know what price to sell them at.

For this, you need to know how much each treatment will **cost *you*** to do.

Many business owners base their prices solely on what their competitors are charging, and although you should always take this into consideration, you need to do your sums independently and let them lead the way, so that the prices you charge work for you. You certainly don't want to be charging less than the cost of the products and time used for your treatments!

The simplest way to do this is to contact the suppliers of your products, as they've often worked out how many treatments you'll get out of each product and an approximate price to charge per treatment. However, do be aware that they may be sparse with their treatments-per-product calculations in order to make the profit margin sound more fabulous than it is! For example, a supplier could tell you that an eyelash tint will cost you £1.40 in products, but you must also take into consideration the disposable add-ons such as cotton wool and bed roll. You would then add on your wage, desired profit and overheads to give you a price that you should be charging.

There are several ways to break down how much to charge for your treatments, but I find the following method to be the most effective...

If you want to work out the *actual* costing of each treatment you must know your **fixed, direct, indirect** and **labour** costs.

Fixed and **direct costs** are the expenses you can specifically connect to a particular treatment. For example, if you are carrying out a simple waxing treatment, your **direct** costs would be:

- Rent/rates (you cannot perform this treatment without a place to work)
- Salary (either your own salary, or that of your employees)
- Stock (wax, spatulas, pre wax cleanser, after wax cream, wax strips, gloves)
- Licence (you may not be able to trade without a licence)

To work out what to charge, you will need to know the following:

- Rent/rates per annum
- Wages per hour (your own or that of your staff)
- National Insurance contributions

- VAT
- Trading hours/days
- The number of work stations

Once you know these figures, you can break it all down and do the sums!

For example, let's say you want to work out the cost of a one hour waxing service, which we'll base on a fictitious salon with fixed costs and overheads as follows: (Please note, for ease of calculation, I have indicated that the salon will open for 52 weeks. Please deduct as appropriate for holidays.)

Rent and rates	£10,000 per year
Wages per hour	£8.00
Employers NI contributions	13.8%
VAT	20%
Trading hours/days	40 hours over five days
Number of work stations	Five

Please note: NI contributions and VAT are subject to change.

So here goes…

Rent
Your £10,000 rent should be divided by the number of workstations in your business. As per our example, our salon has a total of five workstations, which means each workstation must generate an income of at least £2,000 per year.

Next, you need to take the number of days you'll be trading each week (in this case, five), and multiply that by 52 (weeks in the year), which equates to 260 days overall.

Therefore, 260 trading days multiplied by 8 hours per day = 2,080 trading hours per year.

Based on this, each workstation must make at least 96p each and every hour to cover the rent (£2,000 divided by 2,080 hours = 96p)

That bit was nice and easy!

Stock
The next aspect to take into account is the stock you will use for each treatment.

Begin by writing down a detailed list of all the stock you'll need to perform each task (refer back to your treatment list). Find out the size and its price, and be sure to add on the despatch costs and the VAT.

You'll now need to estimate how many treatments you can expect to complete with each product. As previously advised, you could ask your supplier for guidance on this, or you can use your own experience to make a realistic estimate. Ask yourself, if you buy a 500ml bottle of product, will that service five clients or 500? Once you have an idea, divide the price you pay by the number of treatments it will cater for to work out the cost of the product per treatment.

Use the example below as a guide.

Item	Size	Price	Usage	Cost per use
Wax		£4.00	20 clients	£0.20
Spatulas	Box 100	£1.00	20	£0.05
Pre-wax cleanser	1 litre	£4.00		
	30 clients			
	£0.13			
Afterwax oil/lotion	1 litre	£4.00	30 clients	£0.13
Wax strips	100	£2.00	100	£0.02
Total				**£0.53**

Once you have the cost per use, add up the figures to give you the total cost of products for that treatment.

The next step is to add on the wages, including National Insurance contributions. For example, NI contributions at the time of writing are 13.8%, so £8.00 per hour + 13.8% = £9.10

Once you've done this, add all of the figures you have for each section together, and you should have something that looks like this:

Rent/Rates	£0.96
Stock	£0.53
Wages/NI Contribution	£9.10 (per hour)
Total	**£10.59**

You now know that the direct costs of a one hour waxing treatment are £10.59

Next, add up all of your indirect costs for the year and divide them by 2,080 - the number of hours you will trade. These are your overheads - which consists of everything else you pay out to run your business such as:

Expenditure	Monthly	Annually
Insurances	£40	£480
Heat/Light/Power	£150	£1800
Motoring expenses	£40	£480
Travelling and entertainment	£30	£360
Printing and postage	£20	£240
Telephone	£25	£300
Office stationery	£20	£240
Accountancy fees	£140	£1680
Professional fees	50	£600
Repairs and renewals	£10	£120
Loan repayments	£0	£0
Cleaning and laundry	£20	£240
Bank charges and interest	£60	£720
Website maintenance	£10	£120
Salon software	£30	£360
Advertising	£25	£300
Total	£670	£8040

After working out your indirect costs, divide them by your total number of trading hours, and then by the number of workstations you have (in this case 2,080 and five respectively). This will give you a figure of how much you need to make per hour, per workstation.

Let's say the indirect costs for this salon are approximately £8,040 per year.
£8,040 divided by 2,080 = £386.
Divide this by five (workstations) = £0.77

So, each workstation must make £0.77 per hour to cover the indirect costs.

Now you have both the direct and indirect costs for your one hour treatment.

Fixed/Direct costs/Labour costs	£10.59
Indirect costs	£ 0.77
Total	**£11.36**

Now …here comes the hard part!

You'll need to price your treatment so that you actually make a reasonable profit. You certainly don't want to be charging too little that you work at a loss, so getting this bit right is absolutely crucial if you're going to be a successful businessperson!

For the profitability of your business, **mark-up** and **profit margins** are two of the most important calculations you should know.

IMPORTANT!

Mark-up is the percentage you add to your cost price to make a profit.
Profit margin is the percentage profit you make after applying the mark-up.

As a rule of thumb, somewhere between a 40 and 60 per cent mark-up is the average for the hair, nail and beauty industry.

Knowing your profit margins well will also help if you wish to run any discounts or special offers, as you'll need to be certain the adjustments don't impact too much on your profit.

To re-cap, with costs as follows...

Fixed/Direct costs/Labour costs	£10.59
Indirect costs	£0.77
Total	**£11.36**

...you know that the absolute MINIMUM price you can charge for this particular one hour treatment is £11.36

Now that you have your direct and indirect costs worked out, add on your desired mark-up.

In this instance we will price the one hour treatment at £20 which equates to a mark-up of 76.1% and a profit margin of 43.2%.

Suggested mark-up	£08.64
TOTAL COST PER TREATMENT IS	**£20.00**

To work out the mark-up and profit margin percentage, the calculations are as follows:

£8.64 (profit) divided by £11.36 (indirect/direct costs) multiplied by 100 = your **mark-up** percentage.

£8.64 divided by £20 (total selling price) multiplied by 100 = your **profit margin** percentage.

From these calculations you can now decide how much profit you would realistically like to earn.

Desired **profit** to earn:	£115,000
Divide £115,000 by £8.64 (profit)	13,310 treatments per year
13,310 divided by 12 months:	1109 treatments per month
13,310 divided by 52 weeks:	256 treatments per week
256 treatments divided by 5 days:	51 treatments per day
51 treatments per day divided by 5 stations:	10-11 treatments per employee, per day

Of course, this profit is based on all the workstations being busy 100% of the time and its unlikely that your staff could perform 10/11 treatments per day - which would be absolutely fabulous - but is pretty unrealistic! Do the figures again, but work on the assumption that you're busy only 50% or 25% of the time.

> To summarise - add your direct and indirect costs together. Divide the total by the number of hours you will work and then add on your desired percentage for profit and reinvestment. This will give you a price to charge for each treatment.

Share Distribution/Ownership

Share distribution and ownership will only apply if you set up a business as a Limited Company.

'Members' of the company are those who own shares and receive dividend payments, which are payments a company can make to shareholders if it has made enough profit.

Revenue and Sales Forecast

You need to work out how much money you think you will make daily, weekly, monthly and annually.

The aim here is to be realistic with your estimations, so to follow, you'll find a number of revenue examples for a salon, mobile and home based technicians, and for rented space.

Once you've figured out your own approximate figures, you can feed them into your revenue and sales forecast.

Mobile/Home-based/Renting Space

If you're a one-man band, only YOU can generate income into your business.

Begin by writing down the days and hours you'll be working, the price and length of your treatments, and then mock up your output for a 'typical' day.

For example, let's say you're a nail technician who will work four days a week from 9am 'til 4pm. Allow yourself half an hour lunch and two 15-minute breaks throughout the day, which leaves you six hours to make money. Therefore, on a very busy day you could potentially complete...

Three sets of refills	@ £24 each	one hour each
Two gel polishes	@ £20 each	half an hour each
Two full sets of nails	@ £40 each	one hour each

From these figures, you can now estimate that in one six-hour day, working at 100% capacity:

Your Revenue for that day will be = £192

The number of clients seen	= 7
The average spend per client	= £27.42 (£192 divided by 7)

Remember – these calculations are based on you being busy 100% of your day. Work out how much you'd make if you were only busy for 50% - or even just 25% of your day.

For the Salon Owner

If you're a salon owner with staff, your calculations will depend on how many work stations or treatment rooms you have available.

For example, let's say you have five nail desks or hair stations, and that your salon is open for six days a week with five full-time staff.

On average, a member of staff will work eight hours per day. Taking into account half an hour for lunch and two 15-minute breaks throughout the day, this will leave seven full hours to make money. On a very busy day then, each stylist or nail technician has the capacity to complete:

Three cut and colours	@ £80 each	90 minutes each
Two sets of acrylic nails	@ £40 each	One hour each
Five cut and blow dries	@ £40 each	45 minutes each

Your revenue for that day would therefore be £520 per staff member. Once you've multiplied this by five members of staff, you'll discover that your salon has had 50 clients! As a note of caution, remember that these estimates are based on being busy for 100% of your day.

From these figures, you can now estimate that one, seven hour day working at 100% capacity will generate the following figures:

Revenue	= £2,600
Client numbers	= 50

Average spend per client   = £52

Remember these are completely fictitious figures, so be sure to use appropriate figures for your own forecasts so that your assumptions are as realistic as possible.

Assets

An asset is an item of economic value owned by an individual or a business. They are divided into the following categories:

Current assets (i.e. cash)
Long-term assets (i.e. property or equipment)
Pre-paid assets (i.e. future costs such as insurance, rent or interest)
Intangible assets (i.e. trademarks, patents or copyrights)

> **Remember that there is help available to assist you with this area of setting up your business! Don't feel like it's a hurdle you can't jump or be tempted to give up at this point. This is a really important exercise that will give you a clear view of whether or not your business will make money.**

Checklist

Work out your potential revenue.
Produce a cash flow forecast.
Produce a profit and loss forecast.
Show your estimations and calculations and how you came up with your figures.
Establish your break-even point.
Work out your direct and indirect costs.
Cost your treatments.
Produce a balance sheet that shows your assets, liabilities and ownership equity.

Chapter 7

Location and Premises

So … Where Will You Work From?
Salon Owner
Mobile
Home-based
Renting Space
Business Rates
Utility Suppliers
Design, Décor and Layout
Signage

So …where will you work from?

It's crucial that you get the location of your business absolutely spot-on.

Start by writing a list of things that are important to you with regards to where you think your business should be based. For this, go back to your 'vision' to make sure your thoughts about location stay on track with your original goals.

For example, if your dream was to open a swanky salon that provides the very latest facials at £150 a go, there's little point looking in areas with high unemployment. An affluent area with high property prices would be a good indicator that there's expendable incomes to be spent, but ask yourself if the rents in that area of town are going to overstretch you?

Use the internet to do as much research as possible about the areas you're interested in trading in, together with the findings of your market research. Find out if it's an up and coming area…Does it have to be? …Is it a commercial area, or is it conveniently based in your local neighbourhood? …Does your business need to be close to your home or child's school? …Does it need to be on a high street with free local parking, or could it be in a shopping centre?

There's lots to consider here, so be sure to put some serious thought into your potential location and write down the pros and cons of any serious contenders.

Alternatively, like myself, you might have already spotted an empty shop in a great area and started thinking to yourself 'I wonder if…'?

Whatever your rationale for choosing a location, the factors you'll need to consider should include:

- The level of passing trade

- The number of competitors in the area
- Local amenities
- Parking and transport links
- Delivery restrictions

When choosing premises for your business, you have several options available to you.

You could operate from your own home or commercial premises, within an established business, or offer a mobile service. Where you choose to work from can depend upon a number of factors such as your personal commitments and dependencies, your financial situation, or your experience.

<u>Opening a Salon</u>

If opening a salon is your dream, then I would encourage you to go for it!

This would be the most costly, time-consuming and potentially stressful way to set up your business - but if this is your vision, you CAN make it happen.

Here are some important things to consider before deciding to open your very own salon:

- Can you afford it?
- How will you staff it?
- Will your staff be self-employed and renting space from you, or employed by the business? (See 'Staff' on page 135)
- What size salon do you need?
- Do you have the support of family and friends to help you out?
- Can you fully commit to running a business, including its 'out of hours' obligations?

If you've answered a resounding 'yes' to all of these questions, then start searching the web for available premises using commercial estate agents in your desired area. You can also use a property search engine such as Rightmove, or simply drive around the area you're interested in (this was actually how I found my own first salon).

Once you've found potential premises, set up a viewing and arrange to meet up with the landlord or agent. You will need to ask some pertinent questions, so it's essential that you do some appropriate research prior to the meeting. Find out:

- If there is any direct competition nearby? (If so, will that be a problem?)
- If the premises is visible from the road (If not, will this affect custom?)
- If the size of the premises is suitable for your requirements? (Have a clear idea of the space you need for treatments, a reception area, retail space and an area for staff breaks.)
- If the premises are up stairs? (If so, will this make it difficult for potential clients to access the building?)
- If there is there parking nearby?

It is also important to visit the potential property to check out the footfall (passing trade) at different times of the day.

Questions you may want to ask the landlord or agent:

- How much is the rent? Do the figures quoted also include VAT?
- How long is the lease for?
- Is there a break clause (which will allow you to 'break' the lease part-way through)? If so, find out the notice period you will need to give

- Is anybody else currently interested in the property?
- How much deposit will be required to secure the property? (This will often be three months' rent)
- Is there any parking on-site or nearby, and is it free of charge?
- What insurances would you be responsible for? (i.e. buildings, contents and public liability)
- Would you also be responsible for maintaining the outside of the property?
- Is there a gas supply and central heating? (Would this be a problem if there wasn't any?)
- Are the electrics okay?
- What work needs to be done on the property? (Such as decorating, building and joinery)
- Are waste removal costs included in the rates, or would you need to arrange a contract with a private company?
- What planning category is the business currently in?

My one piece of advice here is not to get too excited in front of the landlord or agent, even if turns out to be your dream shop! Take a look around, check the general state of the premises, obtain all the information you need, take plenty of photos (but be sure to ask first!), and politely tell them that you'll be in touch.

Once you've had time to digest everything and work out whether your budget will allow for the rent and shop-fit, and any additional repairs or alterations that are needed, contact your local council and get the necessary information you need from them.

When contacting your local council, be sure to ask the following questions:

- How much are the business rates on the premises? (You will need the business address and postcode for this.)

- Would you be entitled to a small business rates relief?
- Are the correct planning permissions in place for your business?

> Businesses are categorised within the council and a change of use may be necessary for you to trade. This can be both time consuming and costly, and could therefore be a decisive factor in whether or not you decide to pursue your interest in the property. I had to apply for a change of use for my current shop, as although it had formerly been a hairdresser's and was only being changed to a nail and beauty business - the council decided that I didn't fit into a particular category and therefore had to apply for a change of use!

Once you've obtained all the information you need from both the council and the landlord or agent, you can make an informed decision on whether to proceed with the property.

If you're confident that this is 'the one', email the landlord or agent to express your interest. They will almost expect you to negotiate, so have a good think about what you'd like to offer. You may want to try getting the price of the rent down or wish to amend the length of the lease or break clause. You might even want to try your luck at all three!

Remember, **everything** is negotiable and if you don't ask - you don't get, so give it your very best shot.

Before committing to buying or renting commercial premises, make sure you get professional advice from a solicitor. They will understand all the legal jargon connected with the lease and will highlight any areas for concern. Remember to find a reputable solicitor that makes the legal commitments easy to understand - and get a price for the work they'll be doing in advance.

> I managed to get the rent on my first shop reduced by £5000 per year and the break clause reduced from five years to three just by emailing the agent and asking!

Checklist for Opening a Salon

Choose a suitable location.
Complete your desk research.
Find premises and set up viewings if necessary. Don't forget to ask the right questions!
Contact the council regarding business rates, rates relief, planning requirements and waste removal.
Find a solicitor.

Working from Home

This is the most cost effective and convenient way to run your business - but is it professional enough to meet your clients needs? Will your potential clients feel comfortable in your home, or would they actually prefer the salon experience? You should already have a clear indication of this from your market research.

Before committing to working from home, here are some things to consider:

- Your family. This is especially important if you are working inside your family home. Will your family tire of opening the door to a stream of clients?
- Can you keep the children and any pets away from your workspace?
- Ventilation. You will need suitable ventilation if you'll be doing acrylic nails. Add the cost of this to your budget.
- Parking. Will the increase in parking antagonise your neighbours?

- Phone. Don't give out your home phone number! Consider purchasing a 'work' mobile to avoid clients interrupting family time by calling at inconvenient hours.
- Will you need planning permission if you're working from an outbuilding such as a converted garage or summerhouse?
- Will you need to pay business rates on your home?
- Will your landlord or mortgage provider allow it?

Checklist for Home-based Workers

Run your idea by your family.
Contact the local council regarding the payment of business rates.
Contact the Planning Department at your local council to find out if planning permission is required to work from inside your home or an outbuilding.
Contact your mortgage provider or landlord to see if you're permitted to run a business from home.
Contact your insurance company to inform them of your intentions.

Going Mobile

Again, this can be a very cost effective way of setting up and running your business but you must consider the time it'll take to set up at each location, and the impact of travel time on your appointments. For every minute you're setting up, tidying up or travelling - you're not earning.

Take into consideration the findings from your market research, to understand if potential clients are comfortable with having someone in their home to provide treatments.

Things to consider before setting up a mobile business:

- Transport. Do you have a reliable vehicle or will you

need to purchase one?

- Fuel costs and road tax. You must take into account fuel costs, road tax, mileage consumption, wear and tear on your car and any signwriting costs for your vehicle.
- Insurance. You will need a suitable insurance policy that allows you to carry your equipment in your vehicle, which also covers you in the event of theft.
- Parking. Will you have to pay for parking to visit some of your clients?
- Traffic. You must take into consideration traffic problems on your routes (as your entire day could run late as a result of this).
- Unsociable work hours. You may need to make yourself available in the evenings and at weekends in order to build up a solid client base.
- Organisation. You will be responsible for your kit bags being well stocked. You may not be able to carry out your treatments if you find you've run out of something or not packed it.
- Safety.Carefully consider your safety. You may be carrying cash, or possibly visiting unknown clients in their homes, and could also be working until late at night.

Make sure somebody knows where you are and always have your phone charged. Check out new clients as thoroughly as you can by asking questions when they make their first bookings, such as how they heard about you.

Checklist for Mobile Workers

Contact your insurer regarding using your car for business and carrying equipment. You don't want to find yourself uninsured for using the car for work. Think about how much it would cost you to replenish your entire kit if your car got broken into.

Renting Space for the Self-employed

Working within an established business has the obvious advantage of a steady stream of potential clients.

Consider salons, gyms and hotels as possibilities, as salons will already have an established client base, whilst gyms have members and hotels have visitors.

Conduct desk research through Google, Facebook, Instagram etc and compile a list of businesses you would like to work within. Take time to find out the owner/managers name, about the business and its values if you can and search images of their work. Ask yourself if this is a salon that you would like to be associated with.

Prior to the meeting, write a list of questions you'd like to ask. For example:

- How is the rent worked out? Is it a fixed rent, a percentage of your takings, or a combination of both?
- What exactly do you get for your money?
- Is there any furniture included?
- Who washes the towels?
- Are your clients refreshments included in the rent?
- Do you have to work within the established business' opening hours?
- Is there a rent-free period or a discount on rent if you have time off?
- Will you have a key to the premises?
- Will you contribute toward the bills, or are they all inclusive of the rent?
- Will you supply your own products?
- Does the business have a contract for self-employed staff?

There is so much to discuss and some of your questions may seem trivial but remember - there's no such thing as a silly question, so ask them anyway …it could save a lot of hassle in the future!

If the owner doesn't already have one, be sure to get a written agreement drawn up based on the commitments made in your meeting.

There are legal obligations the business owner must uphold with regards to self-employed staff on their premises. Failure to do so could result in huge fines. Speak to your accountant to help clarify this.

Checklist for Renting Space for the Self-employed

Visit the HMRC website for up-to-date information on self-employment guidelines.
Ask your accountant for advice on renting space.

Things to consider before renting space:

- Some business owners may charge you a daily rent which can seem like a daunting figure at first. You could try to negotiate a lower rent for a short period whilst you build up your client base.
- Make sure you have a signed contract or a written agreement (which includes everything you've discussed and agreed on) from the owner to safeguard yourself and your own clients. They may already have one prepared, so don't be afraid to ask.
- Check with your accountant about the stipulations of working within someone else's business. For example, the owner may not be able to dictate the hours you work, advertise for you, make your appointments or handle your takings. You will be your own self-contained business working within

theirs, therefore you must run your business as a completely separate entity.

- Contact your insurance company for advice on working within someone else's business.
- Visit the HMRC website for up-to-date information on self-employment guidelines.

I often hear from disgruntled nail technicians, therapists and stylists who are renting space, complaining about the rent they pay. *"I only get a hair station or a nail desk ...why am I giving the owner a percentage of my wage?"*

If you're considering going down this route, you must understand that owning a business is a huge undertaking with costs ranging from paying the rent or mortgage, business rates, gas, electric and water rates, through to paying the window cleaner, and buying cleaning products, lightbulbs and teabags ...the list really is endless!

Your rent will contribute toward all those things - and bear in mind you won't have the stress of paying for these things like the owner has!

<u>Checklist</u>

Contact businesses you would like to be associated with and put your idea forward.

Arrange a meeting with the manager or the owner.

Clarify EVERYTHING you will be getting for your money.

Find out if there is a set rent, if you'll need to pay a percentage of your earnings, or a combination of the two.

Contact your accountant or a solicitor for their advice on renting space within somebody else's business.

Business Rates

If you decide to open a salon, you will be responsible for paying business rates. These are charged on non-domestic properties and can be paid monthly. If you decide to work from home, you might still be required to pay business rates, so be sure to contact your local council.

Criteria can vary from council to council, but both salon owners and those working from home may be eligible for a business rates relief. Ask your local council for more information on this.

Utility Suppliers

For the salon owner
You will need contracts for your gas, water, electricity, telephone and broadband connection. As you would for a domestic property, search online for the very best deals and compare price packages between companies.

Bear in mind that gas and electricity companies can cause you no end of headaches and interruption as they are desperate for your business. Do be aware that they may try and trick you into believing you are using services without a contract, so deal directly with recognised suppliers and try to avoid brokers.

For the home-based salon
A percentage of your household bills can be taken into consideration when working out your tax. Ask your accountant for advice about this.

If you're renting space
For those of you renting space, check that your rent includes all utilities. You don't want any nasty surprises where the owner announces they expect you to pay half of the electric bill!

We were harassed for several months after opening our salon by gas and electric companies trying to win our business. They told us we were on an emergency tariff and our bills would be thousands of pounds if we didn't sign-up with them straight away. BE WARNED and make certain that you always check your bills. One company took over £1000 from my business account and we hadn't even moved in!

It is also possible to enter a contract verbally, so beware of being misled.

Salon Design, Décor and Layout

Designing your workspace can be very exciting, and now it's time to put all the ideas you've had about how your salon will look into action!

Design and décor
Your salon décor should reflect your businesses personality, incorporate your branding, and take into consideration your target market.

Think carefully about how your colour schemes and interior design will impact upon the type of clients you attract, as even though you might love the idea of a lime green salon - what would an over fifties target market think of such a 'young' colour scheme? If you've always had a particular look in your head, would you need to have a rethink based on the findings of your market research?

When making your decision, make sure you always have your business brand in mind when designing your workspace (see page 98.) There are a plethora of ideas on the internet to inspire you via Google and Pinterest, so keep your clients in mind when making your key design decisions, and consider the atmosphere you are trying to create. Will it be an oasis of calm in a busy city? ...Or perhaps a cool, contemporary salon with designer furnishings for the 40-something professionals? Will it be an Asian-inspired retreat, complete with saris and bamboo for stressed out city dwellers? Or perhaps a cosy home-from-home finished with soft furnishings and the smell of hot, fresh coffee? Whatever you decide, think carefully about what it is you're trying to create before embarking on any costly decorations.

Many companies offer a bespoke design service, but these can be expensive so you would need to be sure whether or not your budget will allow for this. If you see something that you love, consider recreating the 'look' yourself (possibly with the help of a joiner and a decorator) which could be far less expensive. And if you really don't have a clue where to start and can't afford the services of a designer, simply paint it white! You can always add colour later. White is timeless, clean and hygienic-looking, and certainly doesn't have to be stark and boring!

Alternatively, a softer, vintage theme in off-whites or creams is simple to create, and can be teamed with upcycled second-hand furniture to complement your scheme.

Layout
Try to use every inch of your space efficiently, whether you're home-based, renting a spot or opening a salon of your own. Be creative and utilise the space according to the treatments you'll be offering, but don't forget to incorporate a waiting area and reception when planning your layout. This is often the first area your clients will see when they're entering your workplace, so make it as inviting and as professional as possible.

Furniture
Go through your treatment menu and make a list of all the furniture and equipment you'll need to perform the services you will offer. Take into consideration both your client's and your own levels of comfort, as well as style, ease of cleaning and storage facilities. The internet, trade magazines and beauty suppliers are all great places to

look for inspiration.

Don't forget to incorporate your all-important retail space too, preferably in the same spot that your clients will be waiting.

Tradesmen

You may find you require the services of plumbers, builders, decorators, electricians, or shop-fitters. Be clear on the work you require and also get full written quotes, not 'estimates.'

Signage

The presentation of your business offers an important first impression, and your sign is often the first thing passers-by will notice, so it should be the perfect representation of your business.

Look at signage of the shops around you and on the internet for ideas and inspiration, and once you have a good idea of what you'd like to go for, get quotes from local companies. Before pressing ahead with production, ask for a visual of how the finished product will look, as many sign-writers will take a photo of your building or vehicle, and mock-up a computerised image of the sign in situ.

Ensure that the main part of your sign is your business name, and make sure your phone number is clearly written. If your business name doesn't describe exactly what you do, consider having it written underneath, for example:

LUCY BIRCH
MAKE UP ARTISTRY
0111 666 2211

For a salon

Your sign should not need planning permission unless it's illuminated or protruding. For guidance and advice, check this out with your local council.

You could also consider upcycling a sign that's already in place if it's in good condition. Ask your sign writer if this is a possibility.

For the home-based salon

Planning permission would be required to erect a sign outside your house, but stay away from neon or flashing lights, as you don't want to upset your neighbours or the council. Consider a tasteful plaque at your entrance, which will reassure your clients they're in the right place and is unlikely to need planning permission.

If you're renting space

If you are a nail technician working in a hair salon or vice versa, you could consider a wall decal in your own personal space to advertise your micro business within the host business. You can buy these from eBay or you could ask a local graphic designer or sign writer if this is something they offer. Of course, if you're a hairdresser working within a hairdressing salon, you wouldn't need to do this.

Mobile

You should have your car professionally sign written, or you may want to consider magnetic sign-written plates to attach to your car. Make sure your sign lets people know who you are and what you do, and that your contact details are clear. Again, ensure your signage complements your brand and company image.

Checklist

Research the location you want to trade in.
Decide on premises.
Start negotiations if you are renting premises.

Find and set up viewings for premises.

Phone your local council for information on business rates (even if you're working from home), planning requirements and signage.

Start designing your workspace, layout and décor.

Research utility suppliers.

Research signage options and find a sign writer.

Chapter 8

Marketing and Promoting your Business

Your USP
Your Brand
Business Name
Logo
Marketing
Social Media
Promoting your Business

Your USP

Your Unique Selling Point is something that will make you stand out from the competition, so think about what you can do differently to make your business unique.

This can be difficult in industries such as hair, beauty and nails where there are often lots of businesses providing the same services as you, but don't be discouraged. This is about finding your niche and discovering ways to make your business stand out.

Be as original as possible with your ideas but be prepared to be copied!

A great concept that has taken you an age to research and put into place will be copied almost immediately if it's a good one. This can be deflating, flattering and infuriating in equal measures!

From your market research, you should have an idea of how many others are offering the same services as you in your area. Now have a think about how many there are within a 5-mile radius. If your social media followers are friends with those other businesses too, imagine what they're seeing on their newsfeeds every day. Yep, the exact same treatments you're offering! Be original, be creative with your ideas and be unique.

For example, what do you want to be known for?

- Being the cheapest?
- Being the most luxurious?
- Using the highest quality products and treatments?
- Being the friendliest?
- Offering the best treatments?
- Offering the best customer service?

Using your market research, ask yourself what your clients want from you? Are they looking for convenience, quality brands, exceptional customer service or fast treatments? Will your USP fit in with your vision, or might you need to make some alterations? Whatever the outcome, include your findings and decisions in your business plan.

Your Brand, Business Name and Logo

It's important to create the right impression of your business through your branding, business name and logo, so take the time to carefully consider your brief.

Business brand
Branding is the process of creating your business name and its image in your client's minds. The aim is to establish a significant presence that attracts and retains a loyal client base, whilst reflecting your businesses personality - so write a list of words to describe your vision. Is it luxurious, clinical, fresh, modern, eclectic or funky?

Design your brand with some key words in mind, and once you've got some strong, solid branding in place, you can begin to incorporate it into other aspects of your business. For example, if your salon is called 'Angels Nails & Beauty', you could rename your deluxe manicure 'Heavenly Hand Treatment' and design the rest of your treatment titles around your theme. Do beware though, that what may seem quite cute or 'quirky' to you can be off-putting to others. Some people could also find 'themed' price lists difficult or lengthy to read as every treatment might need to be explained.

Business name
Choosing a suitable name can be more difficult than you think!

Start by writing a list of words relevant to your business and have a play around with alternatives (a thesaurus might be useful at this point). Go back to your notebook for inspiration and ask friends for their help and feedback.

Once you've decided on a name, consider developing a tagline …this is a meaningful statement that captures the essence of your brand.

top to toe professional beauty

Luxurious treatments in the comfort of your own home

Your business name certainly doesn't need to be based upon your personal name, and in many cases, using your own name could prove to be detrimental should you wish to sell your business in the future.

Check if the business name is available by visiting the Companies House website, searching social media and checking out the Patent Office at www.ipo.gov.uk. Unless the name is trademarked this shouldn't cause you too many problems. For example, if you want to call your business 'Heavenly Nails' and you're based in Bradford but you find there's a Heavenly Nails in London, you could consider Heavenly Nails by (your name) or Heavenly Nails (your location).

Business logo

Now that you have your business name, you can design your logo, which will be the foundation of your brand. It should sum up everything about your business and be instantly recognisable.

Your business cards, price lists, website and all your promotional materials should integrate your logo and communicate your brand effectively - think Coca Cola, Costa Coffee and M&S – which are all strong brands with instantly recognisable logos.

Ideally, you should work closely with a graphic designer, as a logo designed by yourself on a laptop is unlikely to look polished or professional. Have a look at different websites and social media pages to see what you like and make a note of why you like them. An amazing app recommended to me is *Fiverr*, where you can get your very own logo designed for under a fiver!

Your company name and logo can be protected by a registered trademark to ensure that no one else uses it. It can also be worth money if your business is a roaring success in the future, so go to www.ipo.gov.uk for more information.

Marketing

You need to find a simple way to communicate your ideas to your target audience, which involves so much more than simply handing out your price lists and creating a Facebook page.

Telling potential clients what you do, is in essence, exactly what marketing is all about. Put simply, a successful marketing campaign informs the public what you have to offer and keeps them informed – over and over again.

Your message needs to stand out from that of your competitors, be memorable, and should encourage existing and potential clients to take action. It should be constantly updated throughout the lifecycle of your business, so get off to a flyer and start planning your launch, promotional materials and advertising campaigns now!

Marketing strategies
In its simplest form, your marketing strategy is how you are going to market your treatments, services and products to customers.

Every time you talk about your business, you are marketing. Every price list you give out is marketing.

Planning an actual strategy will depend on where you want your business to go, so write down your aims. You could produce your strategy for the next three months or three years, but a simple way to do this would be to follow the steps bellow:

1. Start with your business goals and be as specific as possible.
2. Next, give each of your goals a realistic deadline.
3. Ask yourself what methods you'll use to advertise and promote these?
4. Figure out if you'll need any marketing materials - such as price lists, vouchers or posters.
5. Ask yourself how you'll track the success of your campaign?
6. Consider how much it'll cost to execute these activities? Will you need posters, leaflets or a 'boost' to your social media activities?

Examples of these targets could be to:

- Acquire more clients
- Improve customer loyalty
- Increase sales
- Encourage word of mouth recommendations
- Generate more 'likes' on Facebook

Aim:	Acquire 500 more Facebook likes.
Deadline	31 August
Frequency	Daily post
Distribution	Facebook
	Twitter
	Instagram
How	Add link and ask people to share. Run competition
Materials	Photo of own work.
Outcome	Gained 380 more likes.

Aim:	Boost Twitter followers by 100.
Deadline	30 September
Frequency	Daily tweets
Distribution	Facebook
	Twitter
	Instagram
How	As above
Materials	As above.
Outcome	Gained 102 new followers.

Aim:	Get 10 new brow wax clients.
Deadline	05 October
Frequency	
Distribution	To regular clients.
How	Offer all regular customers a half price wax
Materials	Poster to display.
Outcome	Nine clients took me up on the offer.

Aim:	Attract five new clients
Deadline	10 October
Frequency	
Distribution	Local
How	Introduce self to local businesses. Offer an introductory offer with a 'use by' date
Materials	Vouchers
Outcome	Result! Got seven new clients.

Make sure every goal is SMART:

- Specific – You'll have a higher chance of accomplishing an explicit goal than a general one
- Measurable – How will you quantify the progress of your goal?
- Achievable – Are your goals attainable?
- Realistic – Are you willing and able to make your goal a reality?

- Time – Set yourself a deadline to achieve your goal

Promoting your business

You need to think creatively about promoting your business and letting people know you're there. Too many people these days rely solely on social media to acquire clients, when you could be out there making a connection in person, meeting your neighbours, shop and bar owners.

You could start off by emailing the people you interviewed for your market research, and give them a discount on their first visit as a goodwill gesture for their time. You should also contact the press or your local community correspondent, or enlist the help of a local PR company.

Also think pro-actively about places that are filled with local people, such as mother and toddler groups, local schools, ladies evenings, prom nights and wedding fayres. Also consider a launch party and invite the press along too.

The list of possibilities is endless and the more you campaign, the better the chance you have of getting clients through the door. Word of mouth is EVERYTHING and potential clients are everywhere …so all you need to do is find them.

It's also essential that you always deliver on your promise, as your clients won't return if your skills aren't up to scratch – and if it's a negative experience, you can guarantee they'll tell all their friends and family about it. Remember, the best type of recommendation is word of mouth, so if you claim to be 'the best nail technician or hairdresser in town', you'd better make sure you are!

Your aim should always be to deliver exceptional treatments that exceed the clients' expectations and you will have a far higher chance of success.

Social Media

Customers expect you to have a presence on social media, and this form of marketing allows you to let the world know who you are and what you do – mostly free of charge.

First of all, you need to figure out what you want your social media to do for you. Do you want to:

- Drive traffic to your website?
- Find out more about your clients?
- Engage with your customers and allow them to ask questions?
- Use it as a networking tool for business contacts?

Whatever your aim, choose the social media platforms that suit your requirements and make sure you save all of your usernames and passwords in a safe place as it can all get very confusing!

Update your social media daily to keep your profiles fresh and relevant but beware - updating your pages can take up hours of your day, especially if you find yourself easily side-tracked!

Consider trying Hootsuite, Tweet Deck or Sprout Social, which will help you manage multiple social media pages all from one convenient place. Here's a quick overview of the business advantages of the major social networks...

Facebook is a social networking site where you can set up a business page to promote your business, so take advantage of this and keep your personal and business profiles separate! You can pay for Facebook adverts relatively cheaply to help grow your audience base by selecting relevant geographical, age and gender demographics to suit your target market.

Twitter is an online social network where users can send and read short messages. This is best used to promote your offers, share photos of your treatments and to run competitions. If there's a major trend, think about how you can link your treatments to the topic on everyone's minds so you can engage the hashtag to its full potential.

Instagram is a free photo and video sharing site to showcase your work with your followers.

LinkedIn is aimed at business professionals for building contacts and sourcing new products and suppliers.

Pinterest is an online notice board where you can share photos of your work and add inspiration boards.

Blogging and Vlogging

A blog is your own personal space where you can share your passions on a regular basis. It can be as light-hearted or as formal as you want it to be, and can be used to review products, deliver your thoughts on the world, offer advice, and to share your work and knowledge.

Always remember to link your blogs to your website and social media accounts – but make sure you check all your spelling and grammar before posting anything - and always keep it professional! You should also be aware that the only way to generate avid followers of your blog is to write genuinely engaging content - and to do so on a regular basis. This will require a reasonable investment of your time, so consider this carefully before making a commitment to a blog.

Vlogging (Video blogging) is relatively simple to set up, just as long as you have something to video yourself with, an internet connection and something interesting you want to say. Video yourself doing make up tutorials, nails, simple hair styles, new massage techniques or the perfect French polish. As with blogs, these may take some time, so be sure that your investment pays off by linking your vlogs to your social media accounts and website. If you have the confidence to do this on a regular basis, also consider setting up your very own YouTube channel.

www.tumblr.com
www.blogger.com
www.wordpress.com
www.youtube.com

Website

For some clients, your website will be their first point of contact with your business. It will give potential customers an idea of what your business is all about and offer an insight into who you are. It's important to get the look and feel of your website just right, and that you use your branding to best effect as this is a golden opportunity to entice new customers.

At the very minimum your website should incorporate:

- Your logo
- Contact details
- Opening hours
- Your location, including a map
- An overview of your business
- Your treatment menu, including a current pricelist

You could also consider:

- Showcasing photographs of your work
- Including links to your social media updates and blogs
- Having an online shop
- Promoting your 'How to' videos

Website and Graphic Designers

Do your research when sourcing website and graphic designers, by looking at their previous work.

Make sure you get an exact price for building your site and don't be tempted to overcomplicate the design as this'll make it difficult to navigate. Remember that first impressions really do count, so be sure to brief your website designer so your site reflects your business image perfectly. There are lots of beautiful website ideas on the internet to inspire you.

Design and Printing

You will need stationary for your new business. Have a graphic designer mock up your business cards, price lists, letter headed paper and gift vouchers incorporating your logo and contact details. Make sure these fit your brand image perfectly and be sure to proof read them before going ahead with printing.

Checklist

Work out your USP.
Decide on your brand identity.
Choose a business name.
Find a web designer.
Design your logo.
Write up your marketing strategy.
Set up your social media accounts.
All stationary designed and printed.

Chapter 9

Your business and the Law

Introduction
Licences
Sale of Goods and Services
Data Protection
Health and Safety
Record Keeping
Planning Permission
Insurance

Making certain you are legally and lawfully compliant is your responsibility as a business owner.

Licences

In the UK there are several licences that are required for you to trade.

Special treatment licences

Some councils require a Special Treatments Licence for certain treatments, such as semi-permanent make-up, ear piercing, aesthetics, manicures and massages amongst others. Check up on this early in the planning stages as it could also impact upon your salon layout and budget.

Contact your local council and speak to both the Health and Safety Department and the Licensing teams to clarify whether you need one or all of these licences, and how much they will cost. Please be aware that you could face a heavy fine if you begin to operate without the correct licences.

Music licences

You will also need licences if you intend to play music to the public, and there are two organisations you need to contact for this.

The PRS (Performing Right Society) collect and distribute money for the use of the music and lyrics on the behalf of the authors, songwriters, composers and publishers. To arrange a licence, contact them at www.prsformusic.com.

PPL (Phonographic Performance Limited) collect and distribute money for the use of recorded music on behalf of record companies and performers. Contact them at www.ppluk.com to arrange a licence.

For royalty free music, try companies such as www.incompetech.com.

> The Government website has a licence finder to clarify which licences you require for different trades. Although it has not yet been updated to include beauty therapy or nail services, hairdressing IS covered. Visit www.gov.uk and search 'licence finder'.

Laws

As a business owner providing treatments or selling products, you should familiarise yourself (and your staff if applicable) with legislation relating to the sale of goods and services, Data Protection, and Health and Safety.

The Sale of Goods and Services
Under the Sale of Goods Act 1979, goods must be as described, of satisfactory quality and fit for purpose.

The Supply of Goods and Services Act 1982
As above, this act covers the Sale of Goods, but also includes legislation about standards of service.

The Sale and Supply of Goods Act
This act requires goods to be described accurately without misleading the customer in any way.
This act amended the two previous acts by introducing guidelines and a definition on 'quality of service'.

Trades Description Act 1968 (revised 1982)
This act protects customers from misleading descriptions or claims relating to treatments and retail products.

The Consumer Protection Act 1987
This piece of EU legislation protects customers when buying goods or services to ensure that all products used during the treatment, service and sale to the client, are safe.

Data Protection Act 1998

This act requires you to comply with the rules regarding the storage and security of all data relating to client records, such as client consultation and record cards.

Having a strict and robust process for keeping client record cards and consultation forms is an important part of your business, so familiarise yourself with the Data Protection Act 1998 to see how this affects you.

Anyone who possesses personal information must comply with the eight principles below, by making sure the information is:

- Fairly and lawfully processed
- Processed for specified purposes
- Adequate, relevant and not excessive
- Accurate and up-to-date
- Not kept for longer than necessary
- Handled according to peoples data protection rights
- Secure
- Not transferred outside of the European Economic Area

More information can be found at www.gov.uk/data-protection.

There are specific rules about storing client and staff information on a computer. For more information and to check if you need to notify the Information Commissioners Office (ICO) go to ico.org/for_organisations/data_protection/registration/self-assessment.

<u>Health and Safety</u>

Wherever you decide to work from, you must take your Health and Safety responsibilities seriously to protect yourself, your clients and your staff.

You must familiarise yourself, and comply with Health and Safety legislation - the main piece being the Health and Safety at Work Act 1974. This places general duties on employers, employees and the self-employed. You can find this on the HSE website at www.hse.gov.uk.

If you employ five or more staff, you are required by law to have a written Health and Safety policy.

In these litigious times, I suggest that anybody running a business in the hair, nail or beauty industry complies with this.

To do so, you are required to have:

- A Health and Safety Policy
- A Health and Safety Procedure Manual
- A Health and Safety Law poster

The Health and Safety Policy:
A Health and Safety policy sets out your general approach and commitment to work-related wellbeing, together with the arrangements you've put in place for managing health and safety across your business.

It will only be effective if it is acted upon and followed by you and your staff.

Your policy will be made up of three parts:

- A statement of intent (What you plan to do to ensure your Health and Safety policy is adhered to)
- Organisation details (Who will be involved)
- Arrangements (How you will prepare, engage and execute your Health and Safety policy)

The Health and Safety Procedure Manual:
Your procedures manual should identify all potential risks in the salon and set out clear procedures on how to prevent and handle them effectively. It should cover the following areas:

- Risk Assessments
- Induction Training
- The salon's environmental conditions
- Storage
- Electrical equipment
- First Aid
- Workplace ergonomics
- Hazardous substances
- Fire Safety and Emergency Evacuations

Up-to-date information and guidance is available at www.hse.gov.uk.

Habia is the Hair and Beauty Industry Authority and I strongly suggest you purchase a copy of their Code of Practice to help you on your way. This is an important booklet for anyone running a hair, nail or beauty business as it sets out specific standards for our industry. The booklet covers everything from infection control and hygiene to salon safety and First Aid.

There's also a pack available to purchase that covers every aspect of Health and Safety. This will guide you through producing your own Health and Safety Policy, and includes forms for you to complete for Risk Assessments, Fire Risk Assessments and COSHH (the Control of Substances Hazardous to Health).

Health and Safety is a specialised, complex area and one which should not be overlooked. The Habia pack puts everything in plain English, and includes everything you need to know - saving you lots of time and unnecessary stress in the long run. You can find out more about Habia at www.habia.org.

> I found the whole process of Health and Safety overwhelming and time consuming. I didn't know what I needed or where to find the information, so I enlisted the help of a specialised consultant who cost me a small fortune and wasted even more of my time! Take heed of the advice in this section, and you'll have everything you need to move forward hassle-free!

<u>Insurance</u>

It's important that you protect your business, your clients, your staff and yourself, so you must make sure you're adequately insured when providing treatments.

Depending on where you work, you will need different types cover, the two most significant being:

Public Liability Insurance which protects you against claims made by the public or visitors on your premises.
Employers Liability Insurance which will protect you against any claims made by employees arising from injuries or negligence obtained at work.

Others types of insurance required may include:

Product Liability if you sell products with your business' name on.
Buildings Insurance which may be the responsibility of either your landlord, or yourself if you own the building. If you're leasing the building, the landlord may ask you to contribute to the cost.
Contents Insurance which covers the cost of theft or damage of equipment, stock and contents.
Vehicle Insurance to cover the protection of carrying products and equipment if you are mobile.

If you're renting space
If you're running your business within someone else's premises but

are operating as your own entity, your insurance is your responsibility. Don't assume you'll automatically be covered by the owner's policy!

Mobile
Make sure you're adequately covered when providing treatments in someone else's home. You don't want to find yourself being responsible for ruining your client's luxurious leather sofa with nail polish, or spilling hair bleach on their great grandmothers' dining table! Unfortunately, accidents do happen from time to time though, so make sure you've got the correct insurance in place to cover all eventualities.

There are companies that provide industry-specific insurance and many of these advertise in trade magazines. Internet forums are also a great place to ask others who their cover is provided by.

Ensure that if you (or your staff) undertake any further training, that you send a copy of your new certificates to the insurance company so they can update your insurance records. Failure to do this could land you in hot water, as even though you've become qualified to carry out a new service, you may not be insured to do so.

> I cannot stress the importance of accurate record-keeping to comply with your insurance policy, in order to cover you in the event of a customer complaint or claim. Ask your insurance provider for specific information that your record cards should include.

Planning Permission

You may need planning permission from your local council when opening a salon, or even if you're working from your own home. Businesses are categorised within the council and you may find you need to apply for permission to trade in a particular building. As a note of caution, don't assume that you'll fall into the same category as a hairdresser if you are a nail technician or beauty therapist.

Make sure you find out about planning regulations and which category the premises is currently in when visiting properties, as it may affect your decision to take on a particular building.

Home-based workers are advised to contact their local council to check current planning regulations for working from outbuildings or within their home.

<u>Checklist</u>

Speak to your local council to find out if you need a Special Treatments Licence and planning permission.
Organise music licences.
Find relevant insurances.
Familiarise yourself with the Sales of Goods and Services Acts.
Familiarise yourself on the Data Protection Act.
Familiarise yourself with the Health and Safety at Work Act 1974.
Organise all health and safety policies and procedures.

Chapter 10

Running your Business

Paperwork
Taking Money
Record Keeping
Suppliers, Stock & Quality Control
Salon Rules
Making Appointments
Customer Complaints
Salon Software
Operations Manual for Salons

In this section we will go over the basics of operating your business. Planning ahead and setting up procedures will help things to run more smoothly.

Paperwork

Start as you mean to go on with your paperwork, by buying yourself some box files, folders and dividers and creating a simple, organised system that's easy to use. You should be able to locate a particular piece of paperwork easily so I suggest keeping separate, named files for everything.

For starters, you'll be needing files for:

- Invoices paid and unpaid
- Bills paid and unpaid
- Bank statements and accounting
- Insurance documents
- All Health and Safety documents
- Stock orders

Salon Software

There are many software systems available specific to the hair, nail and beauty industry - some better than others. Start by working out what you want your software for.

- Is it for clients to make online bookings?
- Is it so you can send SMS text reminders to your clients?
- Do you want to be able to produce regular reports?
- Do you want to store your client information safely?
- Is it simply required as a computerised diary?

Software is becoming increasingly sophisticated so you need to be clear on its primary purpose before an eager rep bamboozles you with their sales patter, and you wind up signing up for something with functionality that you'll only use 20% of (but will need to pay for over the next 24 months!).

I collected information from companies I saw at a trade show and researched them when I got home. I decided that I didn't want anything overly complicated, and that I didn't want to be paying out a monthly fee. It had to be something that both my staff and I could set up and learn quickly.

Again, I would encourage you to ask for advice on industry forums and social media groups for recommendations.

Choosing your Suppliers

Internet forums, trade shows and industry magazines are all places to start looking for suppliers.

Some tasks to consider during this process include:

- Shopping around for the best deals.
- Finding out whether or not the company you're interested in mirrors your business image.
- Look at companies that offer discounts on bulk buys for all your disposables such as cotton wool, bedroll, acetone, foils and suchlike.
- Once you've chosen your suppliers, contact them for a brochure or register on their website so you can order online. Keep a record of all your passwords!
- Find out what their delivery charges are and how quickly they can deliver.

Ordering Stock

Write an inventory of every product you need from every supplier and in which size. The easiest way to do this is to write a list of the treatments you'll be offering and which products and supplies you'll need for each treatment.

When writing your inventory, keep it simple by having the name of the company and their website, phone number and your account number at the top. You could also include a column to record the date the order was received, and if it was received in full - which helps if parts of the order are out of stock. Have one of these lists for each of your suppliers to keep the ordering process simple.

If you decide to order online, keep all account names and passwords safe. There's nothing more annoying than forgetting them at the point of payment!

Sally Supplier
www.sallsup.co
Tel 0800900800
Account No. 2326GF2

Product	Size	Quantity	Price	Date ordered	Date received
Spatulas	Box of 200	1			
Warm Wax		6			
Wax Strips	Pack of 100	1			
After-wax Cleanser	500ml	2			

Ordering tips

- Try to order once a month to keep delivery charges down.
- For organisational ease, pay for your stock as you order it. You'll know where you're at with your finances then, although some companies do offer

credit terms which could help with your cash flow.
- Don't order too much stock when you're first setting up …you can always order more later on if necessary.
- Prices shown for suppliers are usually excluding VAT, so you'll need to add this on - plus any postage and packaging charges.
- See if there is provision for sale or return. That way you won't need to hold on to any excess stock.
- Keep all receipts for everything you purchase.
- Keep complete records of the stock you order, your invoices, and any late or incomplete orders.
- Find out if your local hair and beauty supplier stocks the products you need in case of emergencies.
- Find out if there is a minimum order cost.

Quality Control tips

- Check-off stock against your order as soon as it arrives.
- Any missing or broken products should be reported to the supplier immediately.
- These companies do sometimes make mistakes - so check your delivery thoroughly.
- Don't throw away invoices with the packaging!

<u>Customer Complaints</u>

It isn't always possible to get everything right all of the time and a client may want to let you know about it.

Complaints can be difficult to swallow, but handled correctly, it's possible to salvage a negative situation, correct the problem, and crucially - keep the client coming back. Having a complaints procedure in place (whatever the size of your business) can also help you stay focused in a situation like this.

It is much easier to deal with the problem if you've thought out a plan of action beforehand. In the first instance, stay calm (even if the customer is irate), listen carefully to what they have to say, and always let them finish talking before initiating a response.

Once the client has finished, acknowledge the problem and apologise. Be sympathetic and certainly not defensive - this is a very real problem to them, and so much so that they have felt the need to complain.

You should always offer to compensate the client in some way – maybe with a free treatment, a partial refund or a voucher. Alternatively you could ask the client how they would like to be compensated and what they might consider an acceptable solution to be. Remember your aim in this situation is to keep the client, so if you simply offer a full refund, you'll probably never see them again.

Afterwards, log the problem, investigate it by finding out how and why it happened, and then deal with the root cause to ensure it is never repeated.

In a salon with staff, I would advise you to have a complaints policy in place that all staff are fully aware of.

Sadly we now live in a litigious time; if a client had a complaint 10 years ago, they would have either let you know about it, or never come back. Unfortunately for us professionals, many now turn to the 'no win no fee' solicitors to report their concerns and the first you know about it is when a letter arrives from their solicitor. If this is the case and it happens to you, contact your insurance company straight away.

Disgruntled clients may also turn toward social media as a way to air their grievances with you, so if this situation arises, STAY PROFESSIONAL! There's a chance others will read how you respond, so think very carefully about what you want the world to see.

Sample complaints form

Client name:
Date of complaint:
Date of treatment:
Therapist name:
Brief synopsis of customer's complaint:
How the complaint was received (telephone/email/in person):
Therapist's version of events:
Your comments:
Compensation offered:
What does the client want done?
Client's response:
What has been done to ensure this doesn't happen again:

<u>Salon Rules for Staff</u>

For any business to run smoothly, there needs to be clear rules and procedures in place for staff, so have a think about realistic expectations and write them down. Having clear policies and procedures will ensure that all staff are fully aware of what is expected of them, leaving any doubt about required standards of behaviour at the door! In a salon this should be included as part of your staff handbook (see page 145).

If you're going to be running your own salon, how would you feel about:

- Staff use of mobile phones?
- Staff eating in the salon?

- Cigarette breaks?
- Client confidentiality and gossip?
- Staff use of social media?
- Salon etiquette?

Rules for Clients

Would you dare to have rules for clients too? It's certainly something well worth considering, as you don't want to put clients off booking with you - but a set of ground rules could help you to avoid problems further downstream.

How do you feel about:

- People bringing children into your workplace, or kids being around your products in their own home?
- Clients using mobiles on loud speaker in a salon environment?
- Clients that bring their friends to wait for the duration of their appointment?
- Clients that repeatedly miss their appointment or turn up late?
- Clients that aren't in when you get there? (mobile)

Making Appointments

There are several ways you can record your client's appointments. There's the good old-fashioned diary if you're a small business, sophisticated computerised booking systems for larger businesses, smartphone apps, and online booking companies such as Treatwell.

Do your research, ask on forums for recommendations from other professionals, and find out if there are any monthly fees before signing up to anything.

Taking Money

Offering clients different ways to pay can increase their overall spend with you.

Cash: Many clients will want to pay you in cash. This is fine as long as you keep it separate to your own money to avoid confusion.

Card machine: You may want to install a card machine for your client's convenience, but be sure to shop around for the very best deals. You will be charged each time a client uses this service (hence the reason some businesses add a small charge on to card payments). Speak to your business bank, as they may recommend a preferred provider.

It's certainly worth having a card machine installed, as clients are often tempted to spend more when paying by card than by handing over cash.

Mobile payments: Many companies now offer a mobile payment service where clients can pay you via an app, on their smartphones, or by using a mobile card reader. This is ideal if you're renting space, working from home or mobile. Examples of these service providers include Izettle, PayPal and Ping It.

Cheques: Don't ever take cheques without a valid cheque guarantee card. Please also bear in mind that you'll be charged by your bank for processing cheques.

Gift Vouchers: If you decide to sell gift vouchers, make sure each one is numbered so you can keep track of them when they're redeemed.

Wages

Paying yourself

Whatever you decide to pay yourself, do make sure your wages are affordable to your business. The biggest mistake that people make in our industry is believing that the money they make is for themselves ....WRONG! You'll also need to put money aside for stock, bills, overheads and tax.

How you pay yourself will depend upon the structure of your business. If you're a sole trader, the easiest way is to 'draw' a set amount each month from your business account. These are simply called drawings.

Keep a record of your drawings for your accountant, who will then advise you on how much you must put aside for your tax bill. Getting into the habit of putting this money into a separate account will soften the blow when the tax bill actually arrives.

If you've set up a limited company and are a director, then you are an employee of that company - and will therefore be paid the same as any other employees that the business has. You may also pay PAYE on your earnings. However, once the business is profitable you will be able to take dividends (a cash lump sum) from your company.

Paying your staff

As an employer you must pay at least the minimum wage and provide all the necessary documents such as wage slips. You are also responsible for PAYE (the deduction of income tax and National Insurance contributions from employees' wages), and I would strongly recommend that you employ a book keeper, payroll company or accountant to oversee this.

For each employee, they will need to know:

- Hours worked
- Rate of pay
- Holidays taken
- Commission earned
- Sick leave

Client Record Cards and Data Protection

Having a strict process for keeping client record cards and consultation forms is an important part of your business. You must familiarise yourself with the Data Protection Act 1998 to see how this affects you.

You are required to keep up-to-date records of treatments performed on every client and you must keep all personal data secure. Computerised records should be password protected and paper records should be stored securely in a locked cabinet.

Properly maintained record cards can be used for:

- Complying with the Data Protection Act
- For the Health and Safety of clients
- Complying with licensing requirements
- Marketing purposes
- For complying with your Insurance Provider's requirements

Ask your insurance company about the information they require you to keep on client records. They may have specific guidelines on tint testing (for lash, brow and hair tinting), glue testing (for lashes, lash lifts and suchlike) and for other professional procedures. My own insurance company insists that our clients sign at every appointment to confirm that they have been given aftercare advice, so do be sure to check with yours on the small print.

Salon Operations Manual

For those of you opening a salon, it's extremely important that you and your staff have a clear set of guidelines on how the salon will function. A Salon Operations Manual is the convenient answer to this as it will ensure standards and procedures are set out on how you want the business to run.

Think about exactly how you would like processes in your salon to be completed, such as:

- How will the telephone be answered?
- What will the 'start of day' procedures be, with regard to opening up, turning on the till, turning on the radio, waxer and so on?
- Cleaning: Who will do it and how often?
- Ordering stock: Who will do it and how will they do it?
- Customer complaints: Who will take charge of the complaint and how will it be handled?
- Salon rules: How will the salon run on a day to day basis?
- Cashing up and banking: Who will do it and how will it be done?
- How will staff book holidays?

Checklist

Using your treatment list, source suppliers for all of your products and disposables.

Write an inventory for every product you order, where it's from, their contact number, your account number, and any other relevant information.

Compile Salon Operations Manuals.

Decide on salon and client rules.

Research and decide on salon software.

Decide on how you will store your record cards.

Chapter 11

Staff

Self-employed versus Employed Staff
Your Responsibilities and Employment Law
The Recruitment Process
New Starters
Induction
Self-employed Staff
Staff Handbook
Checklist

Staff

If you're setting up a salon, you will need to staff it adequately. Firstly, you should work out how many staff you'll need based on your operational hours. To do this, you could try sample rotas to ensure all hours are covered to see which arrangements work best for you.

Self-employed versus employed staff

Next up, you'll need to decide if the staff will be self-employed or employed.

Self-employed staff can rent space from you at a fixed daily rate, pay you a percentage of their earnings, or cover your costs as a combination of the two. You must take your own rent (or mortgage repayments) and overheads into consideration when deciding on the level of rent to charge self-employed staff. There is little point in focusing on self-employed staff if the rent they pay you doesn't cover (or massively contribute to) your overheads. You certainly don't want to be doing all the work yourself just to pay the bills!

Renting space to self-employed staff

PROS	CONS
No wages for you to pay	Limited financial growth for your salon (unless they pay a percentage of takings rather than a fixed rent)
No holiday pay entitlement	An 'every man for himself' environment
No maternity benefits to pay	Getting every aspect of renting to self-employed staff right and being fully compliant with HMRC's rules on this.

PROS	CONS
Regular income from their rent	The risk that self employed staff will look for somewhere offering cheaper rent once their diary is full.
No National Insurance contributions to pay	Self employed staff may not invest their money on further training.

Employing staff

PROS	CONS
Fosters team spirit	Wages and N.I. contributions to pay
Controlled financial growth	Holiday pay
Full control over the business	Maternity pay and maternity leave
	Employment Law to consider
	Threat of staff leaving and taking clients elsewhere

> **Remember:**
> Renting out space must be done properly from HMRC's point of view, so check the necessary criteria with your accountant or on the HMRC website, as there are hefty fines to pay if you get it wrong.

Employing staff - Your responsibilities and Employment Law
The Government has strict guidelines in place on employing staff, and you must familiarise yourself with this when you take on employees.

There's lots to consider, from making sure an employee has a legal right to work in the UK to taking on under sixteens - and everything in between.

Employment Law is a highly specialised area that you simply MUST get right! These laws are often subject to change so it's up to you to keep up-to-date with them. Fortunately, there are people out there that can help guide you through this complex area, such as the organisations that follow.

ACAS are the Advisory, Conciliation and Arbitration Service. They can provide impartial advice to both employers and employees on all aspects of employment law www.acas.org.uk.

Habia (the Hair and Beauty Industry Authority) has an excellent Employment Law Pack that you can purchase for salons. It contains model policies and guidance on everything from employing staff to disciplinary procedures. Find out more at www.habia.org.

www.simply-docs.co.uk has pre-written employment and self-employed staff contracts that you can purchase for under £50.

The Recruitment Process

Now you've decided on the number of staff you need, we now need to look into how you go about finding the right people for your team.

All salon owners need a strong, reliable workforce and high staff retention. Keeping staff turnover to a minimum is one of the biggest challenges for salon owners, so having a simple but thorough recruitment process like the one below can help. Following this methodology should prevent you from employing the wrong type of person!

The process:

- Candidate phones regarding position (this allows us to hear their telephone manner)

- Ideally, the candidate brings their CV to you in person (First impressions always count - even if they're only calling in to drop off a CV)
- Complete trade test one (to determine skill level and attitude)
- Complete trade test two (as above)
- Complete trade test three (by this time, you will see more of their personality and how they interact with clients and other staff)
- Conduct primary interview
- Induction
- Begin employment

Start by writing down your essential and desirable criteria for potential staff. This will help to keep you focused whilst conducting trade tests and primary interviews. Make a note of the experience, characteristics and qualifications you would like your dream team to have. Remember, candidates might not be able to fulfil all of them, but a successful applicant could be offered training to upskill them in some areas, so don't automatically dismiss them if they don't tick every one of your boxes!

You might want to consider their:

- Qualifications
- Technical skills
- Communication skills
- Retail experience
- Experience of working to targets
- Order processing and stock control experience
- I.T. skills

Advertising for staff, and the first point of contact
Advertise your staff vacancies on social media, at job centres, through agencies and in local newspapers and ask that interested parties phone you or the salon.

Have a checklist by the phone that you or current staff can refer to, such as the one that follows.

Be sure to ask the caller some simple questions, including their name, email address, previous experience and age. Fill the checklist in and make a note of your first impression of them on the phone.

Convey the process clearly, explaining that *"you'll be invited to take part in up to three trade tests, and successful applicants will then be interviewed"*. Ask the caller upfront if they're available for full or part time work, as you don't want to get all the way to the interview stage, only to be told they can only do one day a week if that's not what you're looking for.

Callers may also enquire about the rate of pay and commission structure. Establishing this at the point of initial contact could save everybody time and effort in the long run, as you wouldn't want to get to the latter stages of the recruitment process and find they suddenly lose interest.

Name	Email Address	Experience/ Quals	Tel. Manner	Appearance
Sarah	sa%@yahao.orgi	NVQ3 4 years exp.	Good. Very chatty.	Good
Katie	Kat3@hotmail.co	College leaver. Studied NVQ2	Sullen	Said she would send CV by email

Ask the caller to bring their CV into the salon in person, as you'll be able to make a note of their appearance and general attitude …you'll be surprised how many won't even pass this stage!

Once CVs have been submitted and read through thoroughly, set up three files …one labelled 'no', one labelled 'maybe', and one labelled 'yes'. Promptly contact those in the 'no' file by email to thank them for their interest and to inform them they've been unsuccessful. Invite the rest along for a trade test by email and explain what they'll be tested on, together with the date, time and location. You will also need to let them know if they need to bring a model or kit.

<u>The Trade Test</u>

This will allow you to see the technical skill and attitude of the candidate at first hand. Remember that they'll be on their very best behaviour at the first and second trade test, hence the requirement for three!

By the time the candidate gets to their third test, you'll have a much clearer idea of their true personality and work ethic as they become more familiar with you.

Decide in advance what the candidates are being tested on, whether that's a cut, colour, gel polish, or a full set of acrylic nails, and simply mark them out of ten.

Whilst they're performing treatments, also make a note of their timekeeping, hygiene, technique, finished results, attitude to clients and staff, and of course, their punctuality on the day.

Depending on the outcome of the first trade test, you may want to invite candidates back for a second time. You can contact the unsuccessful ones by email explaining the rationale for your decision.

Repeat this process again, but after this occasion, successful candidates should be invited back for an interview. This process may seem excessive but needn't take more than a few hours in total.

The benefits of going through the stages in this manner should hopefully take you a step closer to choosing your dream team!

<u>The Interview</u>

Prior to the interviews, set out a document that you can make notes on to keep you on track. Make a list of all the areas that you want to assess, such as:

Personal presentation	
General attitude	
Personable	
Punctuality	
Knowledge	
Sales experience	
Product knowledge	
Skill level	
Consultation	
Results of trade test	

When interviewing, let the interviewee do most of the talking and ask open-ended questions to encourage them to answer fully.

Questions to ask may include:

- Do you enjoy your job?
- Why do you plan on leaving your current job?
- What can you bring to our salon?
- What is your favourite aspect of your current job?
- Is there any training you would benefit from?

When the interview is over, thank the candidate and tell them that you'll be in touch. If you've followed this process, you should now have a clear idea on the most suitable person for the job. Once you've weighed-up your options and made a decision, contact the successful applicant by telling them you'd like to offer them the position, and inform them of their start date, together with some details about their induction. Email unsuccessful candidates, thanking them for applying and explain the rationale of your decision.

> The best advice I can give you at this stage is to always employ on attitude - not skill level. We can always teach skill, but we cannot teach someone to have the right attitude!
>
> Go with your gut instinct. If you think someone shares your values and will fit in well with your team, this is far more important than whether they have the right qualifications.

So now you've selected the right candidates, I suggest you compile a new starter pack to save time, and to ensure that all parts of the employment process are complete. This will then be added to their personal file.

Their personal file could contain:

- A copy of a Contract of Employment
- A copy of your Staff Handbook
- An induction sheet
- Relevant payroll forms

I suggest you keep a personal file for each staff member containing important information on them.

This can be updated during their employment with you, but do remember that this information must be stored in accordance with the Data Protection Act and kept in a locked filing cabinet if it's a paper copy, or password protected if it's held on a computer.

Name, address and telephone number	
Start date	
Date of birth	
Emergency contacts	
Doctors name and address	
Employment start date	
P45 from previous employer	
Bank details	
Absence records	
Annual leave entitlement	
Copy of contract	
Copy of job description	
Disciplinary actions taken	
Termination of contract	
Copy of certificates	

Induction Process

The staff induction process is vital for all new starters. It's a chance to welcome new members to your team and introduce them to the business.

Having a procedure in place for this will ensure that all staff are introduced to the business and its processes in the same way.

Your staff induction may include:

- An introduction to the business – who you are and what you do
- A 'who's who' including job roles
- A run-through of the salon layout
- Explanation of the dress code
- Explanation of general housekeeping expectations
- Overview of facilities and amenities
- Information on transport and parking

- Explanation of hazard and health and safety and reporting
- Explanation of the First Aid procedure and reporting of accidents
- Explanation of absence and other critical employment procedures
- Overview of emergency procedures
- The sign and return of the employment contract
- Completion of a personal file
- Recording of bank details

Write a receipt based on your induction procedure for new staff to sign once the induction is complete. Make sure you keep a copy of this on in their personal file. For example:

1	I have been shown the salon's Health and Safety Policy	
2	I have been shown the company's Employee Handbook	
3	I have been instructed as to what actions I need to take in the event of a fire or other major emergency	
4	I have been shown the locations of each fire exit	
5	I have been shown the location of the fire assembly point	
6	I have been instructed to report any accident, incident or near miss	
7	I have been shown the accident book and a copy of the internal accident investigation/recording form	
8	I have been informed of how to report any concerns to the management	
9	I have been informed of the location of all First Aid kits	
10	I have been informed as to the name of the First Aiders	

11	I have been informed NOT to operate any equipment for which I have not been trained	
12	I have been informed NOT to clean any equipment for which I have not been trained	
13	The company's Personal Protective Equipment system has been fully explained to me	
14	I have signed for the issue of Personal Protective Equipment	
15	The company's Risk Assessment has been explained to me	
16	I have presented my P45	
17	Procedures for booking holidays and time off have been explained	
18	Sickness and absence reporting procedures have been explained to me	
19	I have completed a personal form	
20	I have been offered the opportunity to ask questions	
21	The dress code has been explained to me	
22	I am aware of where I am permitted to park	

Staff Handbook

A Staff Handbook is an important document to have in your salon and can form part of your employment contract. It is an important communication tool between you and your staff and can be used as a resource for new staff members and as a point of reference for all employees.

The Staff Handbook is your chance to write down EXACTLY how you want your dream business to function. Setting out clear procedures at this point will ensure all staff are fully aware of how you want your salon to run. It should also cover areas such as:

- Job descriptions
- Salon practices and procedures

- Holiday and maternity leave
- Disciplinary procedures
- Grievance procedures
- Sick leave
- Salary details
- Responsibilities to the company
- Overtime policy
- Customer complaints
- Termination of contract
- Dress code

There is help and guidance available on the ACAS website at www.acas.org.uk. You can also download a template at www.simply-docs.co.uk.

Employment Contracts

The following information has been directly sourced from the government website https://www.gov.uk.

'All employees have an employment contract with their employer. This is an agreement that sets out an employee's:

- employment conditions
- rights
- responsibilities
- duties

These are called the 'terms' of the contract.

Employees and employers must stick to a contract until it ends (for example, by an employer or employee giving notice or an employee being dismissed) or until the terms are changed (usually by agreement between the employee and employer). As soon as someone accepts a job offer they have a contract with their employer. An employment contract doesn't have to be written down.

The legal parts of a contract are known as 'terms'. An employer should make clear which parts of a contract are legally binding.

Contract terms could be:

- in a written contract, or similar document like a written statement of employment
- verbally agreed
- in an employee handbook or on a company notice board
- in an offer letter from the employer
- required by law (for example, an employer must pay employees at least the National Minimum Wage)
- implied terms - automatically part of a contract even if they're not written down

An employer must give employees a 'written statement of employment particulars' if their employment contract lasts at least a month or more. This isn't an employment contract but will include the main conditions of employment. A written statement can be made up of more than one document (if the employer gives employees different sections of their statement at different times). If this does happen, one of the documents (called the 'principal statement') must include at least:

- the business's name
- the employee's name, job title or a description of work and start date
- if a previous job counts towards a period of continuous employment, the date the period started
- how much and how often an employee will get paid

147

- hours of work (and if employees will have to work Sundays, nights or overtime
- holiday entitlement (and if that includes public holidays)
- where an employee will be working and whether they might have to relocate
- if an employee works in different places, where these will be and what the employer's address is

As well as the principal statement, a written statement must also contain information about:

how long a temporary job is expected to last

the end date of a fixed-term contract

notice periods

collective agreements

pensions

who to go to with a grievance

how to complain about how a grievance is handled

how to complain about a disciplinary or dismissal decision

Think long and hard about what you would like to include in your contract. There are areas specific to our industry such as a 'non-compete' clause being written into your contract. This may prevent staff members enticing clients away from your salon when they leave, or setting up shop over the road from you! Get advice from an experienced professional and search the internet for ideas on what to include.

For more information on employment contracts, visit https://www.gov.uk/employment-contracts-and-conditions

Final Note

Set up a probation period for new starters as there is nothing worse than realising you've employed the wrong person. If they are hard work from the start, **they will only get worse**, so it's much easier to end their employment at the end of the probation period than find yourself having to implement your disciplinary procedure, or worse still, being taken to a tribunal. Find out what the current probation period should be as this can be subject to change.

Help and advice on this can be found on the ACAS website at www.acas.org.uk and www.gov.uk.

Checklist

Make a decision on the required staffing levels and advertise.
Decide on whether staff should be employed or self-employed.
Compile criteria for trade tests and the interview.
Write up your Staff Handbook and contract or Written Statement of Particulars.
Set up a personal file for staff members.
Write up a staff induction.
Research Employment Law.

Chapter 12

Open Day

Create Some Hype
Simple Tips:

Create Some Hype

Now you have (hopefully) completed all sections of this book that are relevant to you, you should be ready to get up and running. It's time for everything to come together and open the doors on your new venture! This will undoubtedly be a stressful, but exciting time for you.

Go back over the checklist, make sure everything is in place and give yourself a huge pat on the back that you have made it this far. As I previously said, you have far more chance of success if you plan your business out in a clear, methodical way.

You need to create as much hype as possible in the run up to the big day, so get your name out there, run competitions, invite the press, arrange some PR, hammer your social media accounts, tell your neighbours, friends and local business owners, and shout about it to everyone that'll listen!! This is an amazing opportunity to get the place buzzing from the off, so take full advantage of it!

Simple Tips

- Open on a Saturday.
- Don't rely on social media 'events' to send out invitations if you have a launch party. Send out tangible invitations to make people feel special. People can find social media invitations impersonal.
- Make sure the place is gleaming and well stocked.
- Give discount vouchers out as an incentive for people to book their first appointments.
- If you decide on a launch party, consider your potential clients and create an event that will attract them. If you want to appeal to the over fifties, you might not want to book an Ibiza-style DJ for example!
- Perform live demonstrations.
- Encourage social media engagement. Have all your guests 'check in' and encourage them to post photos

on their accounts; whoever's picture gets the most 'likes' wins a prize!

- Be creative with your ideas and make the most of your first day. You won't get this opportunity again (...well, not until you open your SECOND shop anyway!)

Chapter 13

Keeping Motivated!

You CAN do this

The Future

A Final Message

You CAN Do This!

Your business has a far higher chance of succeeding if you plan it out carefully. Be absolutely clear on your vision and go through every aspect of your business plan - especially the financial forecasts, to make sure your idea is both profitable and realistically achievable. If it isn't, and the numbers don't quite stack up, don't give up! In the meantime, continue to be an enthusiastic hobbyist and keep practising your skills until the time is right for you.

If you do decide to go forward with your business idea, set yourself clear objectives with times and measurable outcomes and learn to recognise when you need help. Don't ever be afraid to ask for it. There is so much assistance and advice available out there – most of it for free! We have only touched on subjects in this book to get you started but as your business grows, so will your confidence and knowledge. Join industry forums, find out about networking events in your area and see what your local Chamber of Commerce are offering. There are also specialist Salon Coaches that can guide you through the process of running your business to be found on the internet. Advice is everywhere – take it when and where you can!

Keeping Motivated

It can be difficult to stay motivated at times once you're up and running. You'll have had enthusiasm by the bucket-load when you were planning your business, but this can sometimes wane once the doors have opened.

Things might get off to a slow start, or not go quite as well as you'd initially planned, but don't get discouraged if this happens.

Go back to your marketing plan, be creative with your promotions and shout about your business from the rooftops! It's easy to point the finger towards 'bad luck' when things don't go to plan, but you have the power to take control and re-assess your situation. Take a step back to clearly identify any problems, work out an effective solution and come back fighting.

It can also be easy to find yourself feeling overwhelmed. You'll be tending to clients, making appointments, updating your social media accounts, being a bookkeeper, a marketing executive, and a thousand other things that small business demands the owner to do, but having clear systems and procedures in place will help - as will becoming an expert in prioritising!

Tips for keeping motivated:

- Remind yourself of what it is you are trying to achieve.
- Eat well!
- Set regular times to recharge your batteries. Meet up with friends, hang out with your family, read a good book, and give yourself a chance to unwind.
- Surround yourself with positive forces and like-minded people.
- Whilst it's fabulous to have long-term goals …do be sure to set yourself some smaller ones too - and reward yourself when you achieve them.

The difference between successful people and others is persistence! Persevere always, and put in the effort required to generate positive results.

<u>The Future</u>

Planning and redefining your goals is essential to the growth of your business. Without these goals, your business will be in danger of becoming stagnant. Always be sure to keep up to date with industry trends, developments and education to keep your business fresh, and add any new inspirations to your notes. It will remind you of why you're doing what you're doing!

<u>End Note</u>

Thank you so much for buying this book. I do hope that it's helped to guide you through the process of setting up your business.

My final words of advice to you are to be honest, make your business an interesting one, and be absolutely clear on your dreams. But above all, plan, plan and plan!
Keep an open mind to new learnings, stay focused, make great contacts and keep smiling.

Wishing you love and success,

Julie x

Chapter 14
Checklist

Use the checklist to highlight areas that need your attention or to tick off once they're completed!

1. Market Research
2. Business Plan
3. Bank Account
4. Premises
5. Solicitor
6. Business Mentor
7. Planning Permission
8. Insurance
9. Licenses
10. Signage
11. Décor
12. Furniture
13. Health and Safety Policy
14. Health and Safety Procedures
15. Phone line/internet
16. Utility Suppliers
17. Waste removal
18. Salon Operations Manual
19. Staff
20. Staff Starter Pack
21. Staff Training Plan
22. Contracts for staff/self-employed
23. Accountant/Bookkeeper
24. Appointment system (salon software or diary)
25. Stock
26. Music Licenses
27. All stationary (business cards, appointment cards, price lists, gift vouchers etc)
28. Plan of future marketing and campaigns
29. Social Media Accounts
30. Prepare for Open Day

Printed in Great Britain
by Amazon